Glossary of Terms

Acknowledgements:

I would like to acknowledge the following for their invaluable assistance in putting together this Glossary of Terms. This is a working document and is by no means complete:

Colin Hazel

Dr Charles Lawrence

Tony Laws

Dr Noel Merrick

USGS

Dr Richard George

Dr Steve Appleyard

Alan Lemon

Clark Barlow

Dr Hugh Middlemis

Dr Sandie McHugh

Dr Andrew Fitzpatrick

Christa Loos

Royd Nelson

National Guidelines for Water Recycling (2006)

Last updated: 7th April, 2016

Water Resources: Glossary of Terms

Numeric

1P: Proved gas reserves

2P: Proved and probably gas reserves

3P: Proved, probable and possible gas reserves

A

Abandoned: A dry hole or closed well.

Abandonment costs: The costs associated with abandoning a well or production facility. Such costs are specified in the authority for expenditure and typically cover the plugging of well; removal of well equipment, production tanks and associated installations; and surface remediation.

Abnormal events: A geophysical term to indicate features in seismic data other than reflections, including events such as diffractions, multiples, refractions and surface waves. Although the term suggests that such events are not common, they often occur in seismic data.

Abnormal pressure: A subsurface condition in which the pore pressure of a geologic formation exceeds or is less than the expected, or normal, formation pressure. When impermeable rocks, such as shales are compacted rapidly, their pore fluids cannot always escape and must then support the total overlaying rock column, leading to abnormally high formation pressures. Excess pressure, called overpressure or geopressure, can cause a well to blowout or become uncontrollable during drilling. Severe underpressure can cause the drill-pipe to stick to the underpressured formation.

Abrasion test: A laboratory test to evaluate drilling-grade weighting material for potential abrasiveness. The test measures weight loss of a specially shaped, stainless-steel mixer blade after 20 minutes at 11,00 rpm running in a laboratory-prepared mud sample. Abrasiveness is quantified by the rate of weight loss, reported in units of mg/min. Mineral hardness, particle size and shape are the main parameters that affect abrasiveness of weighting materials. Some crystalline formes of hematite grind to a higher percentage of large particles than do other forms and are therefore more abrasive.

Hematites are harder than barites, grind courser and are more abrasive. Thus, a hematite that is proposed as a weighting material for mud is typically a candidate for abrasion testing.

ABS: Acrylonitrile Butadiene Styrene, a composite material used for bore casing.

Absolute age: The measurement of age in years. The determination of the absolute age of rocks, minerals and fossils, in years before the present, is the basis for the field of geochronology. The measurement of decay of radioactive isotopes, especially uranium, strontium, rubidium, argon and carbon, has allowed geologist to more precisely determine the age of rock formations. Tree rings and seasonal sedimentary deposits called varves can be counted to determine absolute age. Although the term implies otherwise, "absolute" ages typically have some amount of potential error and are inexact. Relative age, in contrast, is the determination of whether a given material is younger or other than other surrounding material on the basis of stratigraphic and structural relationships, such as superposition, or by interpretation of fossil content.

Absolute cap: A cap beyond which there is no intention that the level of water entitlements could be increased.

Absolute permeability: The measurement of permeability, or ability to flow or transmit fluids through a rock, conducted when a single fluid, or phase, is present in the rock. The symbol most commonly used for permeability is k, which is measured in units of darcies or millidarcies.

Absolute volume: The volume a solid occupies or displaces when added to water divided by its weight, or the volume per unit mass. In the field, absolute volume is typically given in units of cubic metres per kilogram (m^3/kg)

Absorption: The process by which substances in gaseous, liquid, or solid form are assimilated or taken up by other substances.

Abstraction: The removal of water from a groundwater reservoir, usually by pumping.

Access Arrangement: Coal seam gas explorers must hold an appropriate title before entering a landholder's property. The titleholder cannot undertake any activity on the title unless they have entered into an access arrangement with the property holder.

Accretion: The mechanism by which partially hydrated cuttings stick to parts of the bottom hole assembly and accumulate as a compacted, layered deposit.

Acid: In common usage, acidic water has a pH less than 7.

Acid sulfate soil (ASS): The common name given to soils and sediments containing iron sulfides, the most common being pyrite. When exposed to air as a result of drainage or disturbance, these soils produce sulphuric acid, often releasing toxic quantities of iron, aluminium and heavy metals.

Acidic deposition: The transfer of acidic or acidifying substances from the atmosphere to the surface of the Earth or to objects on its surface. Transfer can be either by wet-deposition processes (rain, snow, dew, fog, frost, hail) or by dry-deposition (gases, aerosols, or fine to course particles).

Acidic rock: An igneous rock that has a relatively high silica content. Examples are granite and rhyolite.

Acoustic transducer: A device for transforming electrical energy into sound, or vice versa. In sonic logging application, acoustic transducers are usually made of piezoelectric ceramic or magnetostrictive materials, and may be used as either receivers or transmitters in a frequency range between about 1 and 30 kHz. The transducers are excited as either monopoles, emitting or receiving sound in all directions, or dipoles, emitting or receiving in one plane. In ultrasonic logging applications, acoustic transducers are made of piezoelectric ceramic materials, and often are used in alternations transmitter/receiver (pulse-echo) mode, in a frequency range from a few hundred kilohertz to a few megahertz.

Acoustic traveltime: The duration of the passage of a signal from the source through the earth and back to the receiver. A time seismic section typically shows the two-way traveltime of the wave.

Acoustic velocity: The rate at which a sound wave travels through a medium. Unlike the physicist's definition of velocity as a vector, its usage in geophysics is as a property of a medium distance divided by traveltime. Velocity can be determined from laboratory measurements, acoustic logs, vertical seismic profiles or from velocity analysis of seismic data. It can vary vertically, laterally and azimuthally in anisotropic media such as rock, and tends to increase with depth in the Earth because compaction reduces porosity. Velocity also varies as a function of how it is derived from the data. For example, the stacking velocity derived from normal movement measurements of common depth point gathers differs from the average velocity measured vertically from a check-shot or vertical seismic profile (VSP). Velocity would be the same only in a constant velocity (homogeneous) medium.

Acoustic velocity log: A display of traveltime of acoustic waves versus depth in a well. The term is commonly used as a synonym for a sonic log. Some acoustic logs display velocity.

Acoustic wave: An elastic body wave or sound wave in which particles oscillate in the direction the wave propagates. P-waves are the waves studied in conventional seismic data. P-waves incident on an interface at other than normal incidence can produce reflected and transmitted S-waves, in that case known as converted waves.

Acquisition: Obtaining the legal right to test a property for mineral resources and produce any that are discovered. The rights can be obtained by purchasing the entire property (surface and mineral rights), purchasing the mineral rights alone, concession, or leasing the mineral rights.

Acre-foot (acre-ft.): - The volume of water needed to cover an acre to a depth of one foot; equivalent to 43,560 cubic feet; 325,851 US gallons (270,000 Imperial gallons); 1230 m^3 or 1,230,000 ML.

Activated carbon: Adsorptive carbon particles or granules that have a high capacity remove trance and soluble components from solution.

Active volume: The volume of water currently stored that may be released through outlet structures and is equal to the current volume less the inactive volume.

Acute toxicity: Rapid adverse effect (e.g. death) caused by a substance in a living organism. Can be used to define either the exposure of the response to an exposure (effect).

Adsorbed gas (shale gas): The gas accumulated on the surface of a solid material, such as a grain of a reservoir rock, or more particularly the organic particles in a shale reservoir. Measurement of adsorbed gas and interstitial gas, which is the gas contained in pore spaces, allows calculation of gas in place in a reservoir.

Adsorption: - The adherence of gas molecules, ions, or molecules in solution to the surface of solids.

Advection: - The process by which solutes are transported by the motion of flowing groundwater.

Advective transport modelling: A series of techniques that use geostatistical methods to determine fluid and contaminant flow in the subsurface. These techniques are used primarily to study contamination in groundwater in environmental studies.

ADWG: The 2004 edition of the Australian Drinking Water Guidelines, published by the National Health and Medical Research Council and Natural Resource Management Ministerial Council.

Aeolian: Pertaining to the environment of deposition of sediments by wind, such as the sand dunes in a desert. Because fine-grained sediments such as clays are removed easily form wind-blown deposits, aeolian sandstones are typically clean and well-sorted.

Aeolotropy: Predictable variation of a property of material with the direction in which it is measured, which can occur at all scales. For a crystal of a mineral, variation in physical propertys observed in different directions is aeolotropy (also known as anisotropy). In rocks, variation in seismic velocity measured parallel or perpendicular to bedding surfaces is a form of aeolotropy. Often found where platy minerals such as micas and clays align parallel to depositional bedding as sediments are compacted, aeolotropy is common in shales.

Aerate: - To supply air to water, soil, or other media.

Aeration zone: The zone immediately below the land surface where the pores contain both water and air, but are not totally saturated with water. Plant roots can capture the moisture passing through this zone, but it cannot provide water for wells.   Also known as the unsaturated zone or vadose zone.

Aerobic: - Pertaining to, taking place in, or caused by the presence of oxygen.

AHD: - Australian Height Datum. Is the level adopted by the National Mapping Council of Australia at its 29th meeting in May 1971 as the datum to which all vertical control for mapping is to be referred. The datum surface is that which passes through mean sea level at the 30 tide gauges and through points at zero AHD height vertically below the other basic junction points. Elevations are normally expressed as mAHD.

Air drill: To drill using gases (typically compressed air or nitrogen) to cool the drill bit and lift cuttings out of the wellbore, instead of the more conventional use of liquids. The advantages of air drilling are that it is usually much faster than drilling with liquids and it may eliminate lost circulation problems. The disadvantages are the inability to control the influx of formation fluid into the bore and the destabilization of the borehole wall in the absence of the bore pressure typically provided by liquids.

Air line: A small diameter pipe installed in the bore and charged with air for the purpose of measuring the water level.

Air waves: A sound wave that travels through the air at approximately 525 k/s and can be generated and recorded during seismic surveying. Air waves are a type of coherent noise.

Airbourne Electromagnetic (AEM): A form of geophysical surveying well suited and applied to general geologic mapping, as well as to fresh water exploration.

Algae: Chlorophyll-bearing nonvascular, primarily aquatic species that have no true roots, sterns, or leaves; most algae are microscopic, but some species can be as large as vascular plants.

Algal bloom: The rapid proliferation of passively floating, simple plant life, such as blue-green algae, in and on a body of water.

Alignment: The horizontal deviation between the actual bore centre line and a straight line representing the ideal central line.

Alkali: Used in reference to materials that are rich in sodium and/or potassium.

Alkaline: - Has a pH greater than 7, pH modifier in the U.S. Fish and Wildlife Service wetland classification system; in common usage, a pH or water greater than 7.4.

Allogenic: Pertaining to minerals or rock fragments that formed in one location but were transported to another location and deposited. Clastic sediments in a rock such as sandstone are allogenic, or formed elsewhere.

Alluvial aquifer: - A water-bearing deposit of unconsolidated material (sand and gravel) left behind by a river or other flowing water.

Alluvial fan: Fan shaped wedge of sediment that accumulates where a stream emerges from mountains onto a flat area. Typically forms in arid and semi-arid areas and can be an important aquifer.

Alluvium: - General term for sediments of gravel, sand, silt, clay, or other particulate rock material deposited by flowing water, usually in the beds of rivers and streams, on a flood plain, on a delta, or at the base of a mountain.

Alpine snow glade: - A marshy clearing between slopes above the timberline in mountains.

Amalgamation: The dissolving or blending of a metal (commonly gold and silver) in mercury to separate it from its parent material.

Amelioration: The act of making better or the condition of being made better.

Ammonia: A compound of nitrogen and hydrogen (NH_3) that is a common by-product of animal waste. Ammonia readily converts to nitrate in soils and streams.

Amphibolite: A non-foliated metamorphic rock that forms through re-crystalisation under conditions of high viscosity and directed pressure. It is composed primarily of amphibole and plagioclase, usually with very little quartz.

Anaerobic: Pertaining to, taking place in, or caused by the absence of oxygen.

Analytical model: - Equations that represent exact solutions to the hydraulic equation for one- or two-dimensional flow problems under broad simplifying assumptions, usually including aquifer homogeneity. They can be solved by hand, or by simple computer programs, (e.g. WinFlow, TwoDan), but do not allow for spatial or temporal variability. They are useful to provide rough approximations for many application with little effort, as they usually do not involve calibration, (site-specific monitoring data is often not available for those simple problems). This approach can suit most simple, low-complexity modelling studies.

Andesite: A fine-grained, extrusive igneous rock composed mainly of plagioclase with other minerals such as homblende, pyroxene and biotite.

Angle of approach: The acute angle at which a wavefront impinges upon an interface, such as a seismic wave impinging upon strata. Normal incidence is the case in which the angle of incidence is zero, the wavefront is parallel to the surface and its raypath is perpendicular, or normal, to the interface. Snell's Law describes the relationship between the angle of incidence and the angle of refraction of a wave.

Anion: A negatively charged ion. Clay surfaces, groups on polymer chains, colloids and other materials have distinct, negatively charged areas or ions. Anionic characteristic affect performance of additives and contaminants in drilling fluids, especially water muds, in which clays and polymers are used extensively.

Anisotropic: Having directionally dependent properties. For a crystal of a mineral, variation in physical properties observed in different directions ins anisotropy. In rocks, variation in seismic velocity measured parallel or perpendicular to bedding surfaces is a form of anisotropy. Often found where platy minerals such as micas and clays align parallel to depositional bedding as sediments are compacted, anisotropy is common in shales.

Anisotropic formation: A formation with directionally dependent properties. The most common directionally dependent properties are permeability and stress. Most formations have vertical to horizontal permeability anisotropy with vertical permeability being much less (often an order of magnitude less) than normal horizontal permeability. Bedding plane permeability anisotropy is common in the presence of natural fractures. Stress anisotropy is frequently greatest between overburden stress and horizontal stress int he bedding plane. Bedding plane stress contrasts are common in tectonically active regions. Permeability anisotropy can sometimes be related to stress anisotropy.

Anistropy: - The condition under which one or more of the hydraulic properties of an aquifer vary according to the direction of flow.

Annular space: The ring-like space between the bore casing and the outer bore casing or borehole.

Anthracite: The highest rank of coal. By definition, a coal with a fixed carbon content of over 91% on a dry ash-free basis. Anthracite coals have a bright lustre, break with a conchoidal fracture, a semi-metallic lustre and are difficult to ignite. Frequently referred to by the layman as, "hard coal".

Anthropogenic: Having to do with or caused by humans.

Anticline: A fold in the Earth's crust, convex upward, whose core contains stratigraphically older rocks.

Annuli: Plural form of annulus.

Annulus: The space between two concentric objects, such as between the bore and casing or between casing and tubing, where fluid can flow. Pipe may consist of drill collars, drill pipe, casing or tubing.

Anomalous: Different from what is typical or expected, or different from what is predicted by a theoretical model. The difference or anomaly may refer to the measurement of the difference between an observed or measured value and the expected values of a physical property. Anomalies can be of great interest in hydrocarbon and mineral exploration because they often indicate hydrocarbon and mineral prospects and accumulations, such as geologic structures like folds and faults. Geochemical anomalies at the surface of the Earth can also indicate an accumulation of hydrocarbons at depth. Geophysical anomalies, such as amplitude anomalies in seismic data and magnetic anomalies in the Earth's crust, can also be associated with hydrocarbon accumulations.

Anoxic: The condition of an environment in which free oxygen is lacking or absent.

Antialias filter: A filter or a set of limits used to eliminate unwanted portions of the spectra of the seismic data, to remove frequencies that might cause aliasing during the process of sampling an analogue signal during acquisition or when the sample rate of digital data is being decreased during seismic processing.

Anticline: Pertaining to an anticline, an arch-shaped fold in rock in which rock layers are upwardly convex. The oldest rock layers form the core of the fold, and outward from the core progressively younger rocks occur. Anticlines form many excellent hydrocarbon traps, particularly in folds with reservoir-quality rocks in their core and impermeable seals in the outer layers of the fold. A syncline is the opposite type of fold, having downwardly convex layers with young rocks at the core.

Antithetic fault: A minor, secondary fault, usually one of a set , whose sense of displacement is opposite to its associated major and synthetic faults. Antithetic-synthetic fault sets are typical in areas of normal faulting.

ANZECC: Australia and New Zealand Environment and Conservation Council.

Aquaculture: The science of farming organisms that live in water, such as fish, shellfish, and algae.

Aquatic: Living or growing in or on water.

Aquatic ecosystem: Any water environment from small to large, from pond to ocean, in which plants and animals interact with the chemical and physical features of the environment.

Aquifer: A water- bearing rock or sediment in a formation, group of formations, or part of a formation that is capable of yielding sufficient water to satisfy a particular demand.

Aquifer, Confined: An aquifer that is overlain by a confining bed. The hydraulic conductivity of the confining bed is significantly lower than that of the aquifer.

Aquifer, Perched: A region in the unsaturated zone where the soil may be locally saturated because it overlies a low-permeability unit.

Aquifer, Semi-Confined: An aquifer confined by a low-permeability layer that permits water to slowly flow through it. During pumping of the aquifer, recharge to the aquifer can occur across the confining layer. Also known as a leaky artesian or leaky confined aquifer.

Aquifer storage and recovery (ASR): Use of a well or series of wells to inject surface water into an aquifer during wet weather or low demand periods for purposes of withdrawal and use during drought and/or high demand periods.

Aquifer, Unconfined: Also known as water-table and phreatic aquifer. An aquifer in which there are no confining beds between the zone of saturation and the surface. The water table is the upper boundary of unconfined aquifers.

Aquifuge: A geologic unit that is incapable of transmitting water under ordinary hydraulic gradients.

Aquitard (Aquiclude): A geologic unit that is permeable enough to transmit significant quantities of water when viewed over large areas and long periods of time, but is not permeable enough to warrant production bores being placed in it. Clays loams and shales are typical aquitards.

Arenaceous: Describing sandy-textured rock or sediment. Arenaceous does not necessarily imply silica-rich, but rather particles of sand size. 0.625 to 2mm, according to the Udden-Wentworth scale.

Argillaceous: Describing rocks or sediment containing particles that are silt or clay sized, less than 0.625mm in size. Most have a high clay-mineral content, and may contain a sufficient percentage of organic material to be considered a source rock for hydrocarbon.

Arkose: A sandstone that contains at least 25% feldspar. Easily recognised because the feldspar grains are typically pink and angular in shape.

ARMCANZ: Agriculture and Resource Management Council of Australia and New Zealand.

Array: An arrangement or configuration of electrodes or antennae used for resistivity, induced polarization (IP), or other types of electromagnetic surveying. Resistivity arrays typically consist of two current electrodes and two potential electrodes and are distinguished by the relative separations between the electrodes.

Array laterolog: An electrode devise with multiple current electrodes configured in several different ways to produce several different responses. A typical array consists of a central electrode emitting survey current, with multiple guard electrodes above and below it. Current is sent between different guard electrode to achieve great or less focusing. The greater the focusing, the greater the depth of investigation. About five basic measurements are obtained in this way. This hardware focusing may be further improved by software focusing, in which the signals from the basic measurements are superimposed mathematically to ensure proper focusing in a wide range of conditions.

Arroyo: A flat bottom gully with steep sides that is a channel for an intermittent stream.

Artesian: Groundwater which rises above the surface of the ground under its own pressure by way of a spring or when accessed by a bore.

Artesian aquifer: See Confined Aquifer.

Artesian basin: A geological structural feature or combination of such features in which water is confined under pressure.

Artesian bore/well: A bore/well tapping a confined aquifer. Water in the bore/well rises above the top of the aquifer under artesian pressure, but does not necessarily reach the land surface. A flowing artesian bore/well is a bore/well in which the standing water level is above the land surface.

Artificial channel storage: Volume of water in artificial channels. Includes the instantaneous volume of moving water, and any water in structure which are not classed as off river storages, on-river reservoirs or farm dams.

Artificial recharge: Augmentation of natural replenishment of groundwater storage by some method of construction, spreading of water, or by pumping water directly into an aquifer. Includes aquifer storage and recovery (ASR).

ASR: Aquifer Storage and Recovery

Asthenosphere: A portion of the upper mantle that is directly below the lithosphere. A zone of low strength in the upper mantle defines the top of the asthenosphere. This weak zone allows the plates of the lithosphere to slide across the top of the asthenosphere.

Astrobleme: An ancient circular scar on Earth's surface produced by the impact of a meteorite or comet.

Atmospheric deposition: The transfer of substances from the air to the surface of the Earth, either in wet form (rain, fog, snow, dew, frost, hail) or in dry form (gases, aerosols, particles).

Atmospheric pressure: The pressure exerted by the atmosphere on any surface beneath or within it; equal to 14.7 pounds per square inch, 101 kilopascals, 1010 millibars or 10.3 metres of water at sea level.

Atoll: A ring-shaped group of coral islands that are surrounded by deep ocean water and that enclose a shallow lagoon.

ATP: Authority to Prospect.

Attenuation: Reduction in mass or concentration of a compound in groundwater over time or distance from the source of constituents of concern due to naturally occurring physical, chemical and biological processes, such as: biodegradation, dispersion, dilution, adsorption and volatilixation.

Australian drinking water guidelines: The National water quality management strategy: Australian drinking water guidelines 6, 2004 (NHMRC & NRMMC 2004a) (ADWG) outlines acceptable criteria for the quality of drinking water in Australia (see this plan's Bibliography).

Australian height datum (AHD): Australian height datum is the height of land in metres above mean sea level. For example, the AHD is +0.025m at Fremantle.

Automatic flow: Self-regulating flow control system with sensing and operation initiated via electronic, mechanical or hydraulic means without an operator intervention.

Available drawdown: For a particular pump installation this is the distance between the SWL and the pump suction i.e. the depth of water over the pump suction.

Available water: Water potentially available for consumptive or environmental use.

Average discharge: As used by the U.S. Geological Survey, the arithmetic average of all complete water years of record of surface water discharge whether consecutive or not. The term "average" generally is reserved for average of record and "mean" is used for averages of shorter periods, namely, daily, monthly, or annual mean discharges. See also Mean.

AWA: Australian Water Association

B

BTEX: The use of BTEX chemicals (benzene, toluene, ethyl benzene and xyelene) in coal seam gas is banned.

Backflow: Fluid flow in the bore from one zone to another in response to pressure difference between the zones. Any time the bore pressure rises above the average pressure in any zone, backflow will occur. Analysis of build-up test involving backflow is either impossible or extremely difficult and usually requires expert input to determine any useful information.

Background concentration: A concentration of a substance in a particular environment that is indicative of minimal influence by human (anthropogenic) sources.

Backwash: The seaward rush of water down a beach that occurs with a receding wave.

Backwater: A body of water in which the flow is slowed or turned back by an obstruction such as a bridge or dam, an opposing current, or the movement of the tide.

Bacteria: Single-celled microscopic organisms.

Bailer: A tube made from pipe with a valve in the bottom, used to remove cuttings or sediments from the hole.

Banded iron ore: A rock that consists of alternating layers of chert and iron oxide mineral (usually hematite) with the iron oxide in high enough concentrate to be of economic value.

Bank: The sloping ground that borders a stream and confines the water in the natural channel when the water level, or flow, is normal.

Bankfull stage: A height of water in a stream that completely fills the natural channel. If the water rises any higher a flood will occur.

Bank storage: Water held in the stream bank during periods of high flow but which flows back to the stream when the water level in the stream recedes.

Bar: An underwater ridge, usually of sand and/or gravel, that forms from the deposition and reworking of sediments by currents and/or waves. Bars occur in rivers, river mouths and in offshore waters.

Barchan: A sand dune that is crescent-shaped in map view. Barchan dunes form in areas of limited sand supply. They move across the desert floor with their gently sloping convex sides facing upwind and their steeply sloping concave sides facing downwind.

Barometric efficiency: The barometric efficiency of an aquifer is a measure of the competence of the overlying confining beds to resist changes in atmospheric pressure. Thick impermeable confining strata are associated with high barometric efficiencies, whereas thinly confined aquifers will display low values. The barometric efficiency of unconfined aquifers is zero.

Barrier Island: A long, narrow island that parallels a shoreline.

Basalt: A dark-coloured fine-grained extrusive igneous rock composed largely of plagioclase feldspar and pyroxene. Similar in composition to gabbro. Basalt is thought to be one of the main components of oceanic crust.

Baseflow: The sustained low flow of a stream, usually groundwater inflow to the stream channel.

Baseflow recession: The declining rate of discharge of a stream fed only by baseflow for an extended period. Typically, a baseflow recession will be exponential.

Base level: The lower limit of erosion by a stream. Sea level is the ultimate base level. However, lakes can serve as a temporary base level in upstream areas.

Basement: The igneous and metamorphic rocks that exist below the oldest sedimentary cover. In some areas such as shields the basement rocks may be exposed at the surface.

Basic: The opposite of acidic; water that has a pH of greater than 7.

Basic rock: An igneous rock that has a relatively low silica content. Examples are gabbro and basalt.

Basin: See Drainage basin.

Batholith: A very large intrusive igneous rock mass that has been exposed by erosion and with an exposed surface area of over 100 square kilometres. A batholith has no known floor.

Bathymetry: Ground elevations below the water surface.

Bauxite: The principal ore of aluminium. A mixture of aluminium oxides and hydroxides that forms from intense chemical weathering of a soil in typical environments.

Bbl: Barrels

Bbl/d: Barrels per day

BCF or bcf: Billion cubic feet (10^9 cubic feet). While BCF is a unit of volume and PJ is a unit of energy, the calorific value of CSG is such, on the average, that one BCF of gas provides one PJ of energy.

Bed: The ground under a body of water. A layer of sediment or sedimentary rock or stratum. A bed is the smallest stratigraphic unit, generally a centimetre or more in thickness. To be labelled a bed, the stratum must be distinguishable from adjacent beds.

Bed material: Sediment composing the streambed.

Bedrock: Solid rock either exposed at the surface or situated below surface soil, unconsolidated sediments an weathered rock.

Bed sediment: The material that temporarily is stationary in the bottom of a stream or other watercourse.

Bedding: The characteristic structure of sedimentary rocks in which layers of different composition, grain size or arrangement are stacked one on top of another in a sequence with oldest at the bottom and youngest at the top.

Bedload: Sediment that moves on or near the streambed and is in almost continuous contact with the bed.

Bedrock: A general term used for solid rock that underlies aquifers, soils or other unconsolidated material.

Benchmark: A standard or point of reference.

Beneficial use: This term is often used in respect of the useful disposal of vast volumes of water generated during coal seam gas extraction. Often following treatment, optimum disposal paths are those that provide values through irrigation, livestock watering, industrial applications or release to water courses in a manner that benefits the environment.

Benthic: Pertaining to the environment and conditions of organisms living at the water bottom, or benthos. Also called benthonic.

Benthic invertebrates: Insects, molluscs, crustaceans, worms, and other organisms without a backbone that live in, on, or near the bottom of lakes, or oceans.

Benthic organism: A form of aquatic life that lives on or near the bottom of streams, lakes, or oceans.

Bentonite: Is a natural clay-like substance formed from the deposition of volcanic ash in seawater. It is composed of clay minerals, predominantly montmorillonite with minor amounts of other smectite group minerals, commonly used in drilling mud. Bentonite swells considerably when exposed to water, making it ideal from protecting formations from infixion by drilling fluids. Montmorillonite forms when basic rocks such as volcanic ash in marine basins are altered.

Bentonite-buried membrane: A liner constructed by uniformly spreading powdered bentonite, 20 – 50 mm thick, over a smooth, firm and dry channel subgrade. This layer is covered by at least 300 mm of stable earth and compacted.

Bentonite-mud: A clay mineral that is composed principally of three-layer clays, such as montmorillonite, and widely used as a mud additive for viscosity and filtration control. Commercial bentonite ores very widely in the amount and quality of the swelling clay, sodium montmorillonite. Ore of lower quality, those with more calcium-type montmorillonite, are treated during grinding by adding one or more of the following: sodium carbonate, long-chain synthetic polymers, carboxymethylcellulose (CMC), starch or polyphosphates. These help made the final product meet quality specification. Unfortunately, the additives may not remain effective in "the real mud world" when in use at the rig due to hardness ions in the water, high temperature, bacterial attack, mechanical shear-degradation and other factors that can render these additives ineffectual.

Bentonite-sediment sealant: Dry, high swell bentonite in granular form is spread over the channel water surface. This material sinks to form a seal at the base of the channel.

Bentonite-soil blanket: A liner constructed by uniformly spreading powdered bentonite over the surface area of a dry channel. The powder is then mixed into the top layer of soil using a rotary type mixer and compacted to form a 50 – 100 mm thick blanket over the channel section.

Best management practices (BMP's): Structural, non-structural, and managerial techniques recognized to be the most effective and practical means to reduce surface water and groundwater contamination while still allowing the productive use of resources.

Beta-Particle: An electron emitted with high energy and velocity from the nucleus of an atom during radioactive decay.

Bind: To exert a strong chemical attraction.

Bioaccumulation: The biological sequestering of a substance at a higher concentration than that at which it occurs in the surrounding environment or medium. Also, the process whereby a substance enters organisms through the gills, epithelial tissues, dietary, or other sources.

Bioavailability: The capacity of a chemical constituent to be taken up by living organisms either through physical contact or by ingestion.

Biochemical: Refers to chemical processes that occur inside or are mediated by living organisms.

Biochemical process: A process characterized by, produced by, or involving chemical reactions in living organisms.

Biochemical Rocks: A sedimentary rock that forms from the chemical activities of organisms. Organic (reef and fossiliferous) limestones and bacterial iron ores are examples.

Biochemical-oxygen demand (BOD): The amount of oxygen, expressed in milligrams per litre that is removed from aquatic environments by the life processes of micro-organisms. Note: BOD_5 is the BOD measured over five days.)

Biodegradation: Transformation of a substance into new compounds through biochemical reactions or the actions of microorganisms such as bacteria. The process by which complex molecules are broken down by micro-organisms to produce simpler compounds. Biodegradation can be either aerobic (with oxygen) or anaerobic (without oxygen). The potential for biodegradation is commonly measured on drilling-fluid products to ensure they do not persist in the environment. A variety of tests exist to assess biodegradation.

Biodiversity: The variety of life forms, including the plants, animals and microorganisms, the genes they contain and the ecosystems and ecological processes of which they are a part.

Biofilm: Microbial populations that grow on the inside of pipes and other surfaces.

Biological treatment: Biological treatment involves the addition of biological agents to either the channel water or soil layer, which assist in reducing the seepage from the channel. There is also the potential for additional ecological benefits in using biological treatments.

Biomass: The amount of living matter, in the form of organisms, present in a particular habitat, usually expressed as weight-per-unit area.

Biophysical Strategic Agricultural Land (BSAL): Has the best quality soil and water resources and is capable of sustaining high levels of productivity. CSG activities may be approved on these lands based on the decision of an independent panel.

Biosolids: The stabilised organic solids derived from sewage treatment processes.

Biosolids reuse: Reuse involved managing biosolids safely and sustainably to beneficially utilise their nutrient, energy or other values. This may include biosolids beneficially used for agriculture (e.g. fertiliser), soil conditioning, mine rehabilitation, etc.

Biosphere water: The total sum of water on the earth.

Biota: All living organisms of an area.

Bioturbated: An adjective used in reference to a sediment or sedimentary rock. Bioturbated sediments have been disturbed by animals (such as burrowing worms or shell fish) or plant roots. These have penetrated the sediment and disturbed any or all original sedimentary laminations and structures. Bioturbated rocks were disturbed in this way while still in the soft sediment phase of their formation.

Biphasic: Referring to the flow of two immiscible fluids: oil and water; oil and gas; or gas and water.

Bit: The tool used to crush or cut rock. Everything on a drilling rig directly or indirectly assists the bit in crushing or cutting the rock. The bit is on the bottom of the drillingstring and must be changed when it becomes excessively dull or stops making progress. Most bits work by scraping or crushing the rock, or both, usually as part of a rotational motion. Some bits, known as hammer bits, pound the rock vertically in much the same fashion as a construction site air hammer.

Bit box: A container, usually made of steel and fitted with a sturdy lock, to store drill bits, especially higher cost PDC and diamond bits. These bits are extremely costly but often small in size, so they are prone to theft.

Bit nozzle: The part of the bit that includes a hole or opening for drilling fluid to exit. The hole is usually small (around 6mm in diameter) and the pressure of the fluid inside the bit is usually high, leading to a high exit velocity through the nozzles that creates a high velocity jet below the nozzles. The high-velocity jet of fluid cleans both the bit teeth and the bottom of the hole.

Bit record: An historical record of how a bit performed in a particular bore. The bit record includes such data as the depth the bit was put into the well, the distance drilled, the hours it was used "on bottom" or "rotating", the mud type and weight, the nozzle sizes, the weight placed on the bit, the rotating speed and hydraulic flow information. The data are usually updated daily. When the bit is pulled at the end of its use, the condition of the bit and the reason it was pulled out of the hole are also recorded. Bit records are often shared amongst operators and bit companies and are one of many valuable sources of data from offset bores for bore design engineers.

Bituminous Coal: A rank of coal that falls between anthracite and semi-bituminous. The most abundant rank of coal. Frequently referred to by the layman as "soft coal".

Blackwater: Water containing human excrement.

Bloom: An unusually large number of organisms of one or a few species, usually algae, per unit of water.

Blowout: A small saucer- or trough-shaped hollow or depression formed by wind erosion on a pre-existing dune or other sand deposit.

Blow out preventer (BOP): Heavy-duty valves used to stop high-pressure oil or gas flowing from the well hole during drilling operations.

Blue-baby syndrome: A condition most common in young infants and certain elderly people that can be caused by ingestion of high amounts of nitrate, which results in the blood losing its ability to effectively carry oxygen.

Boe: Barrels of oil equivalent

Boed: Barrels of oil equivalent per day

Bog: A nutrient-poor, acidic wetland dominated by a waterlogged, spongy mat of sphagnum moss that ultimately forms a thick layer of acidic peat; generally has no inflow or outflow; fed primarily by rain water.

Boil off: Usually refers to the gases generated during the storage of liquefied gases, such as LNG. LNG boils at slightly below -162 degrees C at atmospheric pressure and is loaded, transported and discharged at this temperature.

Bopd: Barrels of oil per day

Boreal: A climatic zone having a definite winter with snow and a short summer that is generally hot, and which is characterized by a large annual range of temperature.

Bore (Well): A bore or a well is a hole drilled into the ground to enable the extraction of groundwater from an aquifer. The term "well" is commonly used in the oil and gas industries and also in the water industry in some countries to describe the same type of facility. In Australia the term "well" has traditionally been applied to a large diameter bore. However, the terms "bore" and "well" are now used interchangeably in the water industry in Australia. For all intents and purposes the two terms are synonymous.

Bore completion report: The report required to be submitted by stand and territory regulatory authorities on completion of bore construction. Also known as Drill Log or Form A.

Borehole: See Drilled well; Exploratory borehole; Observation borehole; Piezometer; Test well.

Borehole logging: Refers to geophysical logging of a borehole, typically including gamma, and conductivity measurements.

Boron: An inorganic chemical that is a micronutrient for plants with a narrow concentration range between deficiency and toxicity. Water softeners are an important source in wastewaters. The main impact of boron is toxicity to plants after soil accumulation, especially on finer textured, higher pH soils.

Bottom land: See Flood plain.

Bottom-land forest: Low-lying forested wetland found along streams and rivers, usually on alluvial flood plains.

Bottoms up mud sample: A sample of mud from the deepest or current drilling depth of a bore. The term refers particularly to a mad sample that has experienced stagnant conditions at the bottom of the hole, including temperature, pressure and other conditions at that depth. A bottoms up same is common collected after a trip out of the hole of in an influx of formation fluid is suspected.

Boundary Conditions:

Specified Head (or Fixed or Constant Head): Refer to Dirichlet Condition (also known as First Type Boundary).

Specified Flow: Refer to Neumann Condition (also known as Second Type Boundary).

Head-dependent Flow: Refer to Cauchy Condition (also known as Third Type Boundary).

BPEM: Best Practice Environmental Management

Brachistochrone: The fastest route that a seismic ray can travel between two points.

Brackish water: Water with a salinity intermediate between seawater and freshwater (containing from 1,000 to 10,000 milligrams per litre of dissolved solids).

Braided stream: A stream characterized by an interlacing or tangled network of several small branching and reuniting shallow channels.

Breakdown product: A compound derived by chemical, biological, or physical action upon a pesticide. The breakdown is a natural process that may result in a more toxic or a less toxic compound and a more persistent or less persistent compound.

Breccia: A clastic sedimentary rock that is composed of large (over two millimetre diameter) angular fragments. The spaces between the large fragments can be filled with a matrix of smaller particles or a mineral cement which binds the rock together.

Brine: Water that contains more than 35,000 milligrams per litre of dissolved solids. This water contains more dissolved inorganic salt than typical seawater.

BTU: British thermal unit - a unit of heat energy defined as the amount of heat required to raise the temperature of one pound of water by one degree Fahrenheit.

Buffer distances and strips: A transition zone between areas managed for different objectives to minimise detrimental interactions between the two.

Butt: A conspicuous hill with steep sides and a flat top. The top is usually a cap-rock of resistant material. This structure is frequently an erosional remnant in an area of flat-lying sedimentary rocks.

BWRO: Brackish Water Reverse Osmosis

Bypass: The act of passing the mud around a piece of equipment, such as passing mud returns around the shale shaker screens or going around a hydrocyclone device. From a mud-engineering viewpoint, this can be a bad practice because it can allow drill solids to degrade and accumulate as fines to the degree that they might cause mud problems.

C

Cable: A cable on which wireline logging tools are lowered into the bore and through which signals from the measurements are passed. The cable consists of a central section with conductors surrounded by a metal, load-bearing armour.

Cable head: An electromechanical device used to connect an electrical tool string to a logging cable, electrical wireline or coiled tubing string equipped with an electrical conductor. It provided attachments to both the mechanical armour wires (which give logging cable its tensile strength) and the outer mechanical housing of a logging tool, usually by means of threads. The connection to the logging tool results in a good electrical path from the electrical conductors of the logging cable to the electrical contact of the logging tool, and shields this electrical path from contact with conductive fluids, such as certain drilling muds. The basic requirements of most cable heads include providing reliable electrical and mechanical connectivity between the running string and tool string. Another attribute of cable heads is that they serve as a "weak link", so that if a logging tool becomes irretrievably stuck in a well, the operator my intentionally pull in excess of the break strength of the logging cable head, causing the cable to pull out of the cable head in a controlled fashion.

Cable tool drilling: A method of drilling whereby an impact tool or bit, suspended in the bore from a steel cable, is dropped repeated on the bottom of the hole to crush the rock. The tool is usually fitted with some sort of cuttings basket to trap the cuttings along the side of the tool. After a few impacts on the bottom of the hole, the cable is reeled in and the cuttings basket emptied, or a bailer is used to remove the cuttings. The tool is reeled back to the bottom of the hole and the process repeated. Due to the increasing time required to retrieve and deploy the bit as the bore is deepened, the cable-tool method is limited to shallow depths. Though largely obsolete, cable-tool operations are still used to drill holes for explosive charge placement and for some water bores.

Cadmium: A heavy metal that can accumulate in soils and is then taken up through the food chain in plants and animals. Concentrations in recycled waters are generally low; however, saline water and changes to soil pH can release cadmium stored in the soil for uptake by plants.

Cake: The residue deposited on a permeable medium when a slurry, such a s drilling fluid, is forced against the medium under a pressure. Filtrate is the liquid that passes through the medium, leaving the cake on the medium. Drilling muds are tested to determine filtration rate and filter-cake properties. Cake properties such as cake thickness, toughness, slickness and permeability are important because the cake that forms on permeable zones in the bore can cause stuck pipe and other drilling problems. Reduced bore production can result from reservoir damage when a poor filter cake allows deep filtrate invasion. A certain degree of cake buildup is desirable to isolate formations from drilling fluids

Cake thickness: See Wall cake thickness.

Calcareous: A rock or substance formed of calcium carbonate or magnesium carbonate by biological deposition or inorganic precipitation, or containing those minerals in sufficient quantities to effervesce when treated with cold hydrochloric acid.

Calcite: The crystalline form of calcium carbonate and chief constituent of limestone and chalk. Calcite reacts readily with dilute hydrochloric acid (HCl), so the presence of calcite can be tested by simply placing a drop of acid on a rock specimen.

Calcium mud: A class of water-based drilling fluid that utilize dissolved Ca^{+2} as a component. Examples are lime mud, gyp mud and calcium chloride ($CaCl_2$) mud.

Caldera: A large, more or less circular, basin-shaped volcanic depression whose diameter is many times greater than the volcanic vent.

Calibration: The process by which the independent variables (parameters) of a numerical model are adjusted, within realistic limits, to produce the best match between simulated and observed data (usually water-level values). This process involves refining the model representation of the hydrogeologic framework, hydraulic properties, and boundary conditions to achieve the desired degree of correspondence between the model simulations and observations of the groundwater flow system.

Calibration, Initial Conditions: The initial hydrologic conditions for a flow system that are represented by its aquifer head distribution at some particular time corresponding to the antecedent hydrologic conditions in that system. Initial conditions provide a starting point for transient simulations.

Calibration, Steady State: The calibration of a model to a set of hydrologic conditions that represent (approximately) an equilibrium condition, with no accounting for aquifer storage changes.

Calibration, Transient or Dynamic: The calibration of a model to hydrologic conditions that vary dynamically with time, including consideration of aquifer storage changes in the mathematical model.

Calorific Value: The energy contained within a certain mass of material, e.g. gas.

Calliper log: A representation of the measured diameter of a bore along its depth. Calliper logs are usually measured mechanically, with only a few using sonic devices. The tools measure diameter at a specific chord across the bore. Since bores are usually irregular, it is important to have a tool that measure diameter at several different locations simultaneously. Such a tool is called a multifinger calliper. Drilling engineers or rigsite personnel use calliper measurement as a qualitative indication of both the condition of the bore and the degree to which the mud system has maintained hole stability. Calliper data are integrated to determine the vole of the open hole, which is then used in planning cementing operations.

Campylobacter: A group of bacteria that is a major cause of diarrhoeal illness.

Canopy angle: Generally, a measure of the openness of a stream to sunlight. Specifically the angle formed by an imaginary line from the highest structure (for example, tree, shrub, or bluff) on one bank eye level at mid channel to the highest structure on the other bank.

CAP: Catchment Action Plan

Cap: An upper limit for the volume of water available for use from a waterway, catchment, basin or aquifer.

Capacitance log: An in situ record of the capability of the fluid passing through a sensor to store electrical charge. Since water has a high dielectric constant, and therefore capacitance, it can be distinguished from oil or gas. The capacitance, or fluid capacitance log, can identify water and be scaled in terms of water holdup.

Capillary fringe: The zone above the water table in which water is held by surface tension. Water in the capillary fringe is under a pressure less than atmospheric.

Capillary tension: The forces acting on soil moisture in the unsaturated zone, attributable to surface tension effects and pore geometry.

Capillary water: Water drawn upward from the water table by capillary action and held in the aeration zone at pressures less than atmospheric pressure. This water can move slowly and in any direction. While most plants rely upon moisture from precipitation that is present in the unsaturated zone, their roots may also tap into capillary water or into the underlying saturated zone.

Carbonate rocks: Rocks (such as limestone or dolostone) that are composed primarily of minerals (such as calcite and dolomite) containing the carbonate ion (CO_3^{2-}).

Carbonic Acid: A weak acid (H_2CO_3) that forms from the reaction of water and carbon dioxide. Most rain water is a very weak carbonic acid solution formed by the reaction of rain with small amounts of carbon dioxide in the atmosphere.

Cased hole: The portion of the bore that has had metal casing placed and cemented to protect the open hole from fluids, pressures bore stability problems or a combination of these possibilities.

Casing: A tube used as a temporary or permanent lining for a bore:

Surface casing: The pipe initially inserted into the top of the hole, to prevent washouts and the erosion of softer materials during subsequent drilling. Surface casing is usually grouted in, and may be composed of steel, PVC-U, or composites such as ABS or FRP. For flowing bores the surface casing needs to be grouted into a competent formation to control subsurface pressures.

Production casing: A continuous string of pipe (casing) that is inserted into or immediately above the chosen aquifer (see Production zone) and back to the surface, through which water is extracted or injected.

Cataclastic rock: A breccia of powdered rock formed by crushing and shearing during tectonic movements.

Catchment: The physical area of land which intercepts rainfall and contributes the collected water to surface water (streams, rivers, wetlands), or groundwater.

Catchment area: The total area of land upstream of a point of interest that captures water and contributes to the flow of water through that particular point.

Cathode: The negative terminal of an electrolytic cell or battery.

Cation: A positively charged ion.

Cation exchange capacity: The quantity of positively charged ions that a clay mineral or similar material can accommodate on its negatively charged surface, expressed as milli-ion equivalent per 100 g, or more commonly as millequivalent (meq) per 100g. Clays are aluminosilicates in which some of the aluminum and silicon ions have been replaced by elements with different valence, or charge.

Cauchy Condition: Also known as Head-dependent Flow or Third Type Boundary Condition. A boundary condition for a groundwater model where the relationship between the head and the flow at a boundary is specified, and the model computes the groundwater flux for the head conditions applying.

CBM: Coal bed methane

Cement: A solid precipitate of calcium carbonate, silica, iron oxide, clay minerals or other materials that forms within the pore spaces of a sediment and binds it into a sedimentary rock.

Cement grout: A fluid mixture of cement and water of a consistency that can be forced through a pipe and placed as required.

Cementation: The processes through which chemical precipitates form within the pore spaces of a sediment and help bind it into a sedimentary rock.

Cementing: The process of placing a grout into an annular space to provide a permanent seal. Also refers to the method often used to stabilise a lost circulation zone or cavity.

Centraliser: A tool used to centre the casing in the hole.

Centre pivot irrigation: An automated sprinkler system involving a rotating pipe or boom that supplies water to a circular area of an agricultural field through sprinkler heads or nozzles.

Channel: Open channel or flume designed to convey water from an upstream water source to farms. Channels can be categorised as:

Main or major channels whose primary purpose is to convey bulk water from headworks storage or river diversion points into the distribution system; or

Distribution channels whose primary purpose is to deliver water from main channels to individual farms.

The term "Canal" is also used from some main channels and usually forms part of the proper name in these cases, e.g. Cattanach Canal, Mulwala Canal, etc.

Channel bed conductance: The conductance (conductivity divided by thickness) of the naturally forming channel lining (largely due to the depositing of suspended sediment in the water) or, in the event of the removal of this lining, the surface layer resistance.

Channel leakage: Loss of water through the banks and base of a channel via macropores.

Channel lining: Low permeability membrane of concrete, compacted clay, bituminous, plastic or other material placed on the inner face of earthen channel, or within the bank, to reduce water loss by seepage. Earth or other materials may be used as cover to protect linings.

Channel regulator: A permanent structure constructed across a channel and fitted with a means of adjusting the waterway area so as to control he rate of water flow along the channel and/or the upstream water level. Most regulators ore one of two general types which utilise different hydraulic characteristics for specific applications:

Overfall weir where water flows over a weir crest which can be varied in level for changing flow rates

Undershot gate having an adjustable sliding gate allowing flows to pass beneath the gate, the rate of flow being controlled by the size of the opening.

Channel scour: Erosion by flowing water and sediment on a stream channel; results in removal of mud, silt, and sand on the outside curve of a stream bend and the bed material of a stream channel.

Channel seepage: Loss of water from a channel via infiltration through micropores and soil processes (i.e. not via preferential flow through micorpores). Seepage as measured in pondage tests includes a leakage component. Generally the term channel seepage refers to both seeped and leaked water, as the two are not easily separated.

Channelization: The straightening and deepening of a stream channel to permit the water to move faster or to drain a wet area for farming.

Check regulator: Channel regulator for overfall flow where flow adjustment is performed by adding or removing timber drop bars ("drop boards" or "stop logs") to provide a moveable weir crest. Where the regulator includes a step in the channel bed it is referred to as a "check and drop" regulator. Small check regulator on-farm channels are also referred to as "channel stops".

Chemical sedimentary rock: A rock that forms from the precipitation of mineral material from solution. Examples are chert and rock salt.

Chemical Weathering: The breaking down of surface rock material by solution or chemical alteration. Common alteration processes are oxidation and hydrolysis.

Chert: A microcrystalline or cryptocrystalline sedimentary rock material composed of SiO_2. Occurs as <u>nodules</u> and concretionary masses and less frequently as a layered deposit.

Chloramination: Use of chloramines (compounds formed by the reaction of hypochlorous acid or aqueous chlorine with ammonia) as a means of disinfection.

Chloride: Chloride in recycled waters comes from a variety of salts (including detergents) and is present as an ion. In addition to its role in salinity, it can be toxic to plants, especially if applied directly to foliage and aquatic biota.

Chlorinated solvent: A volatile organic compound containing chlorine. Some common solvents are trichloroethylene, tetrachloroetheylene, and carbon tetrachloride.

Chlorination: Use of chlorine as a means of disinfection.

Chlorine demand: The difference between the amount of chlorine added to water and the amount of residual chlorine remaining after a given contact time. Chlorine demand may change with dosage, time, temperature, pH and the nature and amount of any impurities in the water.

Chlorofluorocarbons: A class of volatile compounds consisting of carbon, chlorine, and fluorine (commonly called freons) which have been used in refrigeration mechanisms; as blowing agents in the fabrication of flexible and rigid foams; and, until banned from use several years ago, as propellants in spray cans.

Choke: Jaws used to adjust and control he amount of oil or gas flowing from a well.

Christmas tree: The valves, pipes and fittings installed above ground surface at an oil or gas well site. These control and direct the flow of natural gas or oil produced from the well.

Chronic toxicity: Toxicity that acts over a long period of tie and that typically affects a life stage (e.g. reproductive capacity); it can also refer to toxicity resulting from a long-term exposure.

Chrysene: See Polycyclic aromatic hydrocarbon (PAH).

Cinder Cone: A cone-shaped hill that consists of pyroclastic materials ejected from a volcanic vent.

Cirque: A deep, steep-walled, half-bowl like recess or hollow situated high on the side of a mountain and commonly at the head of a glacial valley; and produced by the erosive activity of mountain glaciers.

Clastic: Rock, such as sandstone, or sediment composed principally of broken fragments that are derived from pre-existing rocks which have been transported from their place of origin.

Clay: A clastic mineral particle of any composition that has a grain size smaller than 1/256 mm. The term is also used in reference to a broad category of hydrous silicate minerals in which the silica tetrahedrons are arranged into sheets.

Cleats: The naturally occurring cracks in coal seams (millimetres or less in width) which hold natural gas.

Climate: The sum total of the meteorological elements that characterize the average and extreme conditions of the atmosphere over a long period of time at any one place or region of the Earth's surface.

CMA: Catchment Management Authority.

C02-e: Carbon dioxide equivalent

Coagulation: Clumping together of very fine particles into larger particles using chemicals (coagulants) that neutralise the electrical charges of the fine particles and destabilise the particles.

Coal: A brown or black sedimentary rock that forms from accumulated plant debris. A combustible rock that contains at least 50% (by weight) carbon compounds.

Coal Gasification: The process of converting solid coal into gas, usually by heating. The gas is then used as a fuel or processed into a chemical or liquid fuel.

Coal Liquefaction: The process of converting solid coal into a liquid fuel such as synthetic crude oil or methanol.

Coal Measure: Refers to the stratification of layers of coal interspersed with strata of other sedimentary materials.

Coal Seam Gas (CSG): Coal Seam Gas, also called Coal Seam Methane (CSM) or Coal Bed Methane (CBM), refers to the gas (principally methane) which is found in coal seams.

Coastal aquifers: Deposits of sand formed along the coast by wind and water.

Coastal Plain: An area of low relief along a continental margin that is underlain by thick, gently dipping sediments.

Codex Alimentarius: A food quality and safety code developed by the Codex Alimentarius Commission of the Food and Agriculture Organization of the united Nations and the World Health Organization.

Coliform bacteria: Group of bacteria whose presence in drinking water can be used an as indicator for operational monitoring.

Collection site: A stream, lake, reservoir, or other body of water fed by water drained from a watershed.

Colony forming units: Colony forming units are a measure of pathogen contamination in water.

Compacted clay: Compacted clay or a compacted earth lining consists of importing (and compacting) soils with have better soil characteristics than the in-situ soil (i.e. low permeability and high resistance to erosion).

Compaction of soils in-situ: This involves the enhancement of in-situ soil characteristics such as stability and permeability using standard compaction techniques.

Complexity: The degree to which a model application resembles, or is designed to resemble, the physical hydrogeological system (adapted from the *model fidelity* definition given in Ritchey and Rumbaugh, 1996). A hierarchical classification of three main complexities in order of increasing complexity: Basic, Impact Assessment and Aquifer Simulator. Higher complexity models have a capability to provide for more complex simulations of hydrogeological process and/or address resource management issues more comprehensively. In this guide, the term complexity is used in preference to fidelity.

Complexity, Aquifer Simulator: An Aquifer Simulator is a high complexity representation of the groundwater system, suitable for predicting the response of a system to arbitrary changes in hydrogeological conditions.

Complexity, Basic Model: With limited data availability and status of hydrogeological understanding, and possibly limited budgets, a *Basic* model could be suitable for preliminary quantitative assessment (rough calculations), or to guide a field programme.

Complexity, Impact Assessment Model: More detailed assessments are possible with an Impact Assessment approach, which usually requires more data, better understanding, and greater resources for the study.

Composite Cone: A cone-shaped volcanic mountain composed of alternating layers of cinders and lava flows. Also known as a stratovolcano.

Comprehensive scenario analysis: A sensitivity analysis approach where the results from performing a wide ranging set of model simulation scenarios are assessed to show likely ranges in aquifer response (however, this approach does not quantify the likelihood of each possible outcome, which requires a stochastic or Monte Carlo analysis)

Commercial withdrawals: Water for use by motels, hotels, restaurants, office buildings, commercial facilities, and civilian and military institutions. The water may be obtained from a public supplier or it may be self-supplied.

Community: In ecology, the species that interact in a common area.

Compressibility: The fractional change in unit volume when subjected to a unit change in stress. Both water and soil exhibit compressibility as does the combination of soil and water when they form a bulk matrix.

Compressor: A mechanical device used to raise the pressure of a gas. Compressors can be axial, centrifugal or reciprocating and are usually powered by electrical motors, steam turbines or gas turbines.

Concentration: The ratio of the quantity of any substance present in a sample of a given volume or a given weight compared to the volume or weight of the sample.

Conceptual model: A simplified and idealised representation (usually graphical) of the physical hydrogeologic setting and our hydrogeological understanding of the essential flow processes of the system. This includes the identification and description of the geologic and hydrologic framework, media type, hydraulic properties, sources and sinks, and important aquifer flow and surface-groundwater interaction processes.

Concrete (reinforced, unreinforced, precast, cast in-situ): A hard surface lining formed by the construction of concrete channel sections either in-situ or elsewhere, which are placed onto the surface of the channel subgrade to form a hard surface and seal the channel.

Condensation: The process in the hydrologic cycle by which a vapour becomes a liquid; the opposite of evaporation.

Conditioning: Agitating the borehole while circulating the drilling fluid to help remove cuttings and other unwanted material.

Conductivity: Hydraulic conductivity is the rate of flow under a unit hydraulic gradient through a unit cross-sectional area of aquifer.

Cone of depression: A depression in the water table or potentiometric surface (in the shape of a vortex or an inverted cone) that develops around a bore/well when it is being pumped. The shape of the cone is influenced by the aquifer parameters of transmissivity and storativity, by the pumping rate of the well and by the areal extent of the aquifer. The land surface overlying the cone of depression is referred to as the area of influence.

Confined aquifer (artesian aquifer) - An aquifer that is completely filled with water under pressure and that is overlain and underlain by material that restricts the vertical movement of water. When tapped by a well, water in confined aquifers is forced up, sometimes above the ground surface.

Confining layer (bed) - A body of impermeable or distinctly less permeable (see permeability) material stratigraphically adjacent to one or more aquifers that restricts the movement of water into and out of the aquifers.

Confluence: The flowing together of two or more streams; the place where a tributary joins the main stream.

Conglomerate: A coarse-grained sedimentary rock composed of fragments larger than 2 mm in diameter. The space between the pebbles is generally filled with smaller particles and/or chemical cement that binds the rock together.

Conjunctive Use: The combined use of surface water and groundwater storage to optimise total available water resources.

Connate: Water included in sediments at the time of deposition.

Concentrate: Concentrate or RO Concentrate is the water containing salts or particulate from the treatment processes that has no beneficial use. Can be called "Reject water" also.

Conservation: The use of water-saving methods to reduce the amount of water needed for homes, lawns, farming, and industry, and thus increasing water supplies for optimum long-term economic and social benefits.

Conservation Zones: Areas covers by the National Parks Estate which includes national parks, nature reserves and indigenous areas. Petroleum and CSG exploration is not allowed in these zones, however, exploration may be allowed in State Conservation Areas.

Consolidated rock: Tightly bound geologic formation composed of sandstone, limestone, granite, or other rock.

Constant head permeameter: A device for measuring the saturated hydraulic conductivity of soils. A constant head of water is maintained in a shallow auger hole and the rate of leakage from the apparatus to maintain this constant head (once saturated conditions have been reached) is proportional to the saturated hydraulic conductivity (or permeability) of the soil.

Constituent: A chemical or biological substance in water, sediment, or biota that can be measured by an analytical method.

Construction: The entire process of creating a bore, from initial drilling and inserting the surface casing through to insertion of a screen and developing the aquifer prior to installing a pump.

Consumer: An individual or organisation that uses drinking water.

Consumptive pool: The amount of water resources that can be made available for consumptive use in a particular water resource plan area under the rules of the water resource plan for that area.

Consumptive use: The use of a resource that reduces the supply (removing water from a source like a river, lake or aquifer without returning an equal amount). Examples include the intake of water by plants, humans, and other animals and the incorporation of water into the products of industrial or food processing.

Contact recreation: Recreational activities, such as swimming and kayaking, in which contact with water is prolonged or intimate, and in which there is a likelihood of ingesting water.

Contaminant: Any substance that when added to water (or another substance) makes it impure and unfit for consumption or an intended use. Biological or chemical substance or entity, not normally present in a system, capable of producing an adverse effect in a biological system, seriously injuring structure or function.

Contamination - Degradation of water quality, compared with original or natural conditions, due to human activity.

Contour Line: A line on a map that traces locations where the value of a variable is constant. For example, contour lines of elevation trace points of equal elevation across the map. All points on the "ten metre" contour line are ten metres above sea level.

Contour Map: A map that shows the change in value of a variable over a geographic area through the use of contour lines. For example, a contour map of elevation has lines that trace points of equal elevation across the map.

Conventional filtration: The process of passing wastewater through a bed of granular media (e.g. sand and anthracite) to remove particulate matter.

Conveyance losses: Water evaporation and seepage from surface water sources and main-made water transportation facilities, such as irrigation channels.

Coral reef: A ridge of limestone, composed chiefly of coral, coral sands, and solid limestone resulting from organic secretion of calcium carbonate; occur along continents and islands where the temperature is generally above 18°C.

Core or Coring: The process of drilling a hole and retaining the material from a target depth for examination and testing – "taking a core".

Core hole: A bore drilled to obtain cores of the underlying geological strata to inform analysis of soil/rock/coal type, strength, permeability, chemical composition and yield.

Core sample: A sample of rock, soil, or other material obtained by driving a hollow tube into the undisturbed medium and withdrawing it with its contained sample.

Core trenching: A mechanism for reducing the seepage from channels by excavating a trench either side of the channel and filling the trench with an imperious substance.

Corrective action: Procedures to be followed when monitoring results indicate a deviation occurs from acceptable criteria.

Covered flexible membrane: The construction of a lined channel using a geomembrane to reduce seepage where the geomembrane is covered with a non-erosive material that protects the geomembrane.

Criterion: A standard rule or test on which a judgment or decision can be based.

Critical control point: A point, step or procedure at which control can be applied which is essential for preventing or eliminating a hazard, or reducing it to an acceptable level.

Critical Industry Cluster or CIC: A concentration of highly productive industries within a region that are related to each other, contribute to the identity of the region and provide significant employment opportunities. Two types of CIC have been identified – equine (horse breeding and training) and viticulture (grape cultivation) industries. CSG activities are not allowed within these clusters.

Critical limit: A prescribed tolerance that must be met to ensure that a critical control point effectively controls a potential health hazard; a criterion that separates acceptability form unacceptability.

Crop coefficient (Kc): Dimensionless coefficient used to calculate evapotranspiration requirement for a particular crop from the potential evapotranspiration for a reference crop (ETo). Crop coefficients are determined experimentally and take into account leaf area development of the crop and the crop canopy physiology.

Crop plants: Plants grown for harvest as food, feed or forage.

Crop water requirement: The total volume of water required to meet the plants requirements for evapotranspiration for a given planting area and period (excluding leaching fraction).

Crude Oil: A liquid hydrocarbon produced from natural underground reservoirs. It might also include liquid hydrocarbons produced from tar sands, gilsonite, and oil shale. Crude oil can be refined into a number of petroleum products which include: heating oil, gasoline, diesel fuel, jet fuel, lubricants, asphalt, ethane, propane, butane, and many other products.

Cryptosporidium: Microorganism commonly found in lakes and rivers that is highly resistant to disinfection. Cryptosporidium has caused several large outbreaks of gastrointestinal illness, with symptoms that include diarrhoea, nausea and stomach cramps. People with severely weakened immune systems (i.e. severely immunocomprised people) are likely to have more severe and more persistent symptoms than healthy individuals.

Crystalline rocks: Rocks (igneous or metamorphic) consisting wholly of crystals or fragments of crystals.

CSG evaporation dam: Defined as any impoundment, enclosure or structure that is designed to be used to hold CSG water for evaporation or would result in greater evaporative loss than the quantity of water being actively processed or treated.

CSG water: Groundwater this is necessarily or unavoidably brought to the surface of the earth, or moved underground in connection with exploring for or producing coal seam gas. CSG water is defined as a waste.

Ct: The product of residual disinfectant concentration © in milligrams per litre determined before or at taps providing water for human consumption, and the corresponding disinfectant contact time (t) in minutes.

Culvert: An underground structure or pipe carrying water beneath a road, carriageway, etc.

Cumulative Distribution Function (cdf): A graph or formula that expresses the probability that an uncertain parameter will be less than or equal to a particular value.

Current volume: The volume of water currently stored.

Curve numbers (CN): Empirical number between 0 and 100 developed by the United States National Resource Conservation Service (NRCS) to compute rainfall losses on now-free ground.

Customer (drainage) collection point: A legitimate water service location that may or may not have a measurement device at which a customer is proved with a rural water services from a rural water deliver agency. This could be either a water supply or a drainage collection point.

Customer service point: A legitimate water service location that may or may not have a measurement device at which a customer is provided with a rural water service from a rural water delivery agency. This could be either a water supply or a drainage collection point.

Customer (water) supply point: A legitimate water service location that may or may not have a measurement device at which a customer is provided with a rural water service from a rural water delivery agency. This could be either a water supply or a drainage collect point.

Cyclone: See Tropical cyclone.

Cyanobacteria: Bacteria containing chlorophyll and phycobilins, commonly known as 'blue-green algae'.

D

Dam: A barrier to obstruct the flow of water, especially one of earth, masonry, etc., built across a stream.

Darcy: A unit of intrinsic permeability. It is not an SI unit, but is used widely in petroleum engineering and in geology. A medium with a permeability of 1 Darcy permits a flow of 1 cm/sec of a fluid with a viscosity of 1 centipoise under a pressure gradient of 1atmosphere/cm. To convert to equivalent values of hydraulic conductivity for water at normal atmospheric conditions, 1 millidarcy (mD) = 8.64 x 10^{-4} m/day.

Darcy's Law: A relationship formulated by Henry Darcy during the mid-1800's which governs the flow of fluids through porous media. Darcy's Law forms the basis of most groundwater flow equations. It is an empirical equation developed to compute the quantity of water flowing through an aquifer. Usually expressed as:

Q=KiA or Q=Tiw, where:

Q = flow,

K= hydraulic conductivity,

I = hydraulic gradient,

A = aquifer cross-sectional area,

T = transmissivity,

w = width of aquifer transverse to flow path.

Datum: A reference location or elevation which is used as a starting point for subsequent measurements. Sea level is a datum for elevation measurements. Datums can also be arbitrary such as the starting point for stream stage measurements or based upon a physical feature such as the base of a rock unit.

Datum plane: A horizontal plane to which ground elevations or water surface elevations are referenced.

DDT: Dichloro-diphenyl-trichloroethane. An organochlorine insecticide no longer registered for use in the United States.

Dead storage: Capacity of a storage that is below the minimum operating level and cannot, under normal circumstances, be supplied to customers. Dead storage can be accessed for emergency supply (i.e. in times of drought) by installing temporary pumps to get the water from below the minimum operating level. The minimum operating level can also be determined by water quality constraints.

Deciduous: Refers to plants that shed foliage at the end of the growing season.

Decollment: A horizontal to sub-horizontal fault or shear zone with a very large displacement. The rocks above the fault might have been moved thousands of meters or more relative to the rocks below the fault. This often produces a situation where the rocks above the fault have entirely different structures than the rocks below the fault.

Decommissioned bore: A bore, the purpose and use of which have been permanently discontinued.

Deep drainage: The volume of water that moves below the root zone which may or may not enter the saturated zone and become recharge to the groundwater system.

Deep lead: A term used by the gold miners of Victoria to describe an aquifer at great depth formed in the sand and gravel that has filled an ancient river valley and been covered by more recent deposits. It may be at depths of up to 60m or more and be several kilometres wide. Deep leads are the major regional aquifers under the Loddon, Campaspe and Goulburn Plains in northern Victoria.

Deepwater habitat: Permanently flooded lands lying below the deepwater boundary of wetlands.

Degradation products: Compounds resulting from transformation of an organic substance through chemical, photo-chemical, and/or biochemical reactions.

Degraded: Condition of the quality of water that has been made unfit for some specified purpose.

Delayed yield: When water is not released instantaneously from storage.

Delta: The low, nearly flat tract of land at or near the mouth of a river, resulting from the accumulation of sediment supplied by various courses of the river in such quantities that it is not removed by tides, waves, or currents. It is commonly a triangular or fan-shaped plain.

DEM: Digital Elevation Model.

Demineralised water: Water of exceptionally high purity from which all salts and minerals have been removed.

Dendritic drainage: A stream drainage pattern that resembles the veins of a leaf in map view. Occurs mainly where the rocks below have a uniform resistance to erosion.

Denitrification: A process by which oxidized forms of nitrogen such as **nitrate** (NO_3^-) are reduced to form nitrites, nitrogen oxides, ammonia, or free nitrogen: commonly brought about by the action of denitrifying bacteria and usually resulting in the escape of nitrogen to the air.

Density: The ratio of mass and volume. Units are kilograms per cubic metre or grams per cubic centimetre.

Density current: A gravity-driven flow of dense water down an underwater slope. The increased density of the water is a result of a temperature difference, increased salinity or suspended sediment load.

Depth averaged flow: Modelling assumption that the hydraulic flow is constant throughout the depth with negligible vertical flow.

Deposition: The settling from suspension of transported sediments, also the precipitation of chemical sediments from mineral rich waters.

Desalination: The process of removing excess salt and other minerals from water in order to obtain freshwater suitable for human consumption and other purposes.

Desert pavement: A ground cover of granule-size and larger particles that is typically found in arid areas. This ground cover of coarse particles is a residual deposit - formed when the wind selectively removes the sand-, silt- and clay-sized materials.

Design storm: A hypothetical storm for a specified storm frequency (return period) used as a standard in the design of hydraulic structures.

Desorption: The process of reversal of absorbtion.

Detect: To determine the presence of a compound.

Detection limit: The concentration of a constituent or analyte below which a particular analytical method cannot determine, with a high degree of certainty, the concentration.

Deterministic: A description of a parameter or a process with uniquely defined qualities. A deterministic parameter has, or is assumed to have, a unique value or a unique spatial distribution. The outcome of a deterministic process is known with certainty. There is, or is assumed to be, a clear cause-and-effect relation between independent and dependent variables.

Dethridge meter outlet: Positive displacement flow measurement device used to determine water volumes supplied from the authority supply channel to an individual farm. The meter consists of a metal wheel fitted with eight vanes around the circumference and mounted on a horizontal axis in a concrete flume emplacement. Water flowing along the flume causes the wheel to rotate and a counting device records the number of revolutions which provides a direct measure of the volume of water supplied over a given time.

Detrital: A word used in reference to sediments or sedimentary rocks that are composed of particles that were transported and deposited by wind, water or ice.

Developed yield: Developed yield should be reported as the total volume of water that could be diverted for use, on average, at existing infrastructure levels over the critical period of interest and at a set level of reliability. The developed yield does not include volumes released for the environment, that is, it is the yield capable of being supplied under current infrastructure development after provisions for environmental flows have been made. For some surface water management areas the developed yield may exceed the sustainable yield.

Development: The removal of sand and other fines (including drilling mud) from the aquifer immediately surrounding the bore and creating a filter zone around the bore that prevents further movement of aquifer particles into the bore.

Development Well: A well drilled within the proven area of an oil or gas reservoir to the depth of the productive stratigraphic horizon. These wells are expected to be productive.

Dewater: The remove water from a waste product, streambed or mine, for example.

Diagenesis: All of the changes which happen to a sediment after deposition, excluding weathering and metamorphism. Diagenesis includes compaction, cementation, leaching and replacement.

Dialysis water: High purity water used for kidney dialysis.

Diatoms: Single-celled, colonial, or filamentous algae with siliceous cell walls constructed of two overlapping parts. Diatoms can occur in very large numbers and can make significant contributions to sea-floor or lake sediment.

Diatomite: A light coloured, fine-grained siliceous sedimentary rock that forms from a sediment rich in diatom remains.

Dieldrin: An organochlorine insecticide no longer registered for use in the United States. Also a degradation product of the insecticide aldrin.

Differentiated planet: A planet that has layers composed of elements and minerals of different densities. As an example, Earth is a differentiated planet because it has a metal-rich core, surrounded by a rocky mantle, and covered by a crust of low-density minerals.

Diffuse source: A diffuse source of pollution originates from a widespread non-specific area (e.g. urban stormwater runoff, agricultural infiltration) as opposed to a particular point source (see point source pollution).

Diffusion: The movement of a substance from an area of high concentration to an area of low concentration. It is often driven by chemistry.

Diffusivity: The diffusivity of an aquifer is the ratio of transmissivity and storage coefficient. It gives an indication of how fast a pressure change can be transmitted or diffused through an aquifer.

Dilution flow: A volume of fresh water used to dilute salty flows.

Diorite: A coarse-grained, intrusive igneous rock that contains a mixture of feldspar, pyroxene, hornblende and sometimes quartz.

Dirichlet Condition: Also known as a Specified, Fixed or Constant Head Boundary, or Third Type Boundary Condition. A boundary condition for a groundwater model where the head is known and specified at the boundary of the flow field, and the model computes the associated groundwater flow.

Direct drinking water (potable) reuse: The discharge of recycled water directly into drinking water treatment facility or into a drinking water distribution system.

Direct feed: A water source that is fed directly to the reverse osmosis process without pre-treatment.

Direct runoff: The runoff entering stream channels promptly after rainfall or snowmelt.

Directional drilling: Drilling wells that are deliberately deviated from the vertical to hit a target that is not directly beneath the well site or to penetrate a greater thickness of rock within a productive zone.

Discharge: An outflow of water from a stream, pipe, groundwater system, or watershed; the opposite of recharge.

Discharge area (groundwater) - Area where groundwater is discharged to the land surface, to surface water, or to the atmosphere.

Discharge rate: The volume of fluid passing a point per unit of time, commonly expressed in litres per second, cubic metres per second, megalitres per day or other convenient unit.

Discretisation: The process of dividing an object into a finite number of elements or portions.

Disinfectant: An oxidising agent (e.g. chlorine, chlorine dioxide, chloramines and ozone) that is added to water in any part of the treatment or distribution process and is intended to kill or inactivate pathogenic (disease-causing) microorganisms.

Disinfectant residual: The amount of free and /or available disinfectant remaining after a given contact time under specified conditions.

Disinfection: The process designed to kill most microorganisms in water, including essentially all pathogenic (disease-causing) bacteria. There are several way to disinfect, with chlorine being most frequently used in water treatment.

Disinfection by-product: Products of reactions between disinfectants, particularly chlorine, and naturally occurring organic material.

Dispersion: The extent to which a liquid substance introduced into a groundwater system spreads as it moves through the system. It is driven by the plumbing of the matrix of the groundwater system

Dissected: Cut by erosion into valleys, hills, and upland plains.

Dissolved constituent: Operationally defined as a constituent that passes through a 0A5-micrometre filter.

Dissolved oxygen: Oxygen dissolved in water. It is one of the most important indicators of the condition of a water body. Dissolved oxygen is necessary for the life of fish and most other aquatic organisms.

Dissolved solids: Minerals and organic matter dissolved in water.

Distributed model: A type of numerical model in which input parameters are discretized into small computational elements across the modelling domain. Distributed models are capable of preserving heterogeneous properties to the extent that these properties can be represented by the computational elements.

Distributed water: Water supplied by water authorities via a distribution network.

Distribution system: A network of pipes leading from a treatment plant to customer's plumbing systems.

Diversion: A turning aside or alteration of the natural course of a flow of water, normally considered to physically leave the natural channel.

Divertible: The ability to extract water from a surface water or groundwater resource, in a given area.

Divide: A ridge that separates two adjacent drainage basins.

DNAPL (Dense Non-Aqueous Phase Liquid): A DNAPL is one of a group of organic substances that are relatively insoluble in water and more dense than water. DNAPLs tend to sink vertically through sand and gravel aquifers to the underlying layer.

Doline (sink hole): A natural depression or hole in limestone caused by its chemical solution.

Dolomite: A sedimentary rock consisting chiefly of magnesium carbonate.

Dome: An uplift that is round or elliptical in map view with beds dipping away in all directions from a central point.

Domestic withdrawals: Water used for normal household purposes, such as drinking, food preparation, bathing, washing clothes and dishes, flushing toilets, and watering lawns and gardens. The water may be obtained from a public supplier or may be self-supplied.

Dominant plant: The plant species controlling a particular environment.

Dose response: The quantitative relationship between the dose of an agent and an effect caused by the agent.

Downstream regulation: A method of channel regulation where the water level is controlled or maintained on the downstream side of the control structure. This control mode often operates automatically as demand signals are passed up the system.

Drainage area: The drainage area of a stream at a specified location is that area upstream of that location which is enclosed by a drainage divide.

Drainage basin: The geographic area that contributes runoff to a stream. It can be outlined on a topographic map by tracing the points of highest elevation (usually ridge crests) between two adjacent stream valleys. Also referred to as a "watershed".

Drainage channel: An open channel or a modified natural waterway designed to remove excess water from rural lands.

Drainage divide: The boundary between two adjacent drainage basins. Drainage divides are ridge crests (or less obvious locations where slope of the landscape changes direction). Runoff produced on one side of the ridge flows into stream "A" and runoff on the other side of the ridge flows into stream "B".

Drainage factor: The drainage factor is a parameter associated with the delayed yield in unconfined aquifers and is similar to the leakage factor for semi-confined aquifers.

It is defined as:

$$B = \sqrt{\frac{Kb}{\alpha S_y}}$$

where:

K = hydraulic conductivity of the aquifer.

b = aquifer thickness.

1/α = the Boulton delay index (an empirical constant).

S_y = the specific yield after a long pumping time.

Large values of B indicate a fast drainage. If B = ∞ the yield is instantaneous with the lowering of the water table, so the aquifer would be confined without delayed yield.

The dimensions of B are in length, and the units are metres.

Drainage network: A collection of network of carriers which is used to convey irrigation induced excess surface water or excess groundwater.

Drainage network carriers: Network carriers are typically unlined channels (i.e. open drains), natural waterways, or buried perforated pipes.

Drainage overpass: Pipe or flume conduit to convey natural drainage flows across supply channel. Used in steep topography where a drainage subway is not practicable.

Drainage runoff: Flow of surface water from a given area resulting from the effects of rainwater and/or applied irrigation water in excess of crop water requirement and leaching.

Drainage subway: Conduit laid transversely under supply channel to convey natural drainage flows across the channel.

Drainage surface diversion service: A rural water service that provides for the diversion of raw water by customers from a surface water source at a specific level of service and which confers common obligations on customers. Typically, service provision involves water access, works or site licence administration, metering or measurement and monitoring of diversions on a regular basis. Aspects of water planning and water resource management may also be involved. Surface diversion services are classified into three sub-categories:

Unregulated: A service that enables customers to pump or divert under specific conditions from a surface water source, typically a stream, that is not regulated or controlled by a structure or structures operated by a rural water delivery agency.

Regulated: A service that enables customers to pump or divert from a surface water source, typically a river that is regulated or controlled by a structure or structures operated by a rural water delivery agency.

Drainage: A service that enables customers to pump or divert from a surface drain operated by a rural water delivery agency. In some circumstances, drainage diversion is included in the surface drainage service and the reporting agency should report against the primary service with explanatory comment provided.

Drawdown: The difference between the water level in a bore/well before pumping and the water level in the bore/well during pumping. Also, for flowing wells, the reduction of the pressure head as a result of the discharge of water.

Drift: A general term for all sedimentary materials deposited directly from the ice or melt water of a glacier.

Drill stem test (DST): A testing procedure to determine the fluid content of a reservoir and its ability to produce.

Drill string: A column of drill pipe lengths screwed together.

Driller: A licensed water bore driller who is ultimately responsible for the work being carried out.

Drilling fluid: A medium used to stabilise the formation, control groundwater, and remove the drill cuttings from the hole as drilling takes place.

Drilling operations: The drilling, construction, development, maintenance and rehabilitation, and decommissioning of a bore.

Drinking water: Water intended primarily for human consumption.

Drinking water quality management audit: The systematic and documented evaluation of activities and processes to confirm that objectives are being met, and which includes an assessment of management system implementation and capability.

Drinking water quality monitoring: The wide-ranging assessment of the quality of water in the distribution system and as supplied to the customer, which includes the regular sampling and testing performed for assessing conformance with guideline values and compliance with regulatory requirements and agreed levels of service.

Drinking water supplier: An organization, agency or company that has responsibility and authority for treating and/or supplying drinking water.

Drinking water supply system (water supply system): All aspects from the point of collection of water to the consumer. This can include catchments, groundwater systems, source waters, storage reservoir and intakes, treatment systems, service reservoirs and distribution systems and the consumer.

Drip irrigation: An irrigation system in which water is applied directly to the root zone of plants by means of applicators (orifices, emitters, porous tubing, or perforated pipe) operated under low pressure. The applicators can be placed on or below the surface of the ground or can be suspended from supports.

Drop structure: Concrete, timber or steel weir structure placed in supply channel or drain to dissipate energy (to minimise erosion) at a point of desired reduction in water levels.

Drought: An extended period with little or no precipitation; often affects crop production and availability of water supplies.

Drilled well: A water well/bore constructed by drilling. Synonyms are tube-well, production well or production bore.

Drumlin: A low, smoothly rounded, elongate hill. Drumlins are deposits of compacted till that are sculpted beneath the ice of a flowing glacier. The long axis of a drumlin parallels the flow direction of the ice.

Dry gas: Natural gas having no liquid hydrocarbons.

Dry hole: A well without significant groundwater or hydrocarbon reserves.

DTM: Digital Terrain Model.

Dune: A mound or ridge of wind-blown sand. Typically found in deserts and inland from a beach. Many dunes are moved by the wind.

Dupuit Assumptions: The following assumptions for flow in an unconfined aquifer:

(a) hydraulic gradient is equal to the slope of the water table,

(b) streamlines are horizontal, and

(c) equipotential lines are vertical.

E

EA: Environmental Authority

Earthflow: A detached mass of soil that moves downslope over a curved failure surface under the influence of gravity. An earthflow is more complex than a slump; it has a higher moisture content and the moving mass of soil has some internal movement or "flow". Rates of movement are typically a few inches per year but faster rates can occur.

Earthquake: A trembling of the earth caused by a sudden release of energy stored in subsurface rock units.

EC: An acronym for Electrical Conductivity unit. 1 EC = 1 micro-Siemens per centimetre, measured at 25°C. It is used as a measure of water salinity (see salinity below).

EC50 (Median effective concentration, 50%): Concentration of a substance in water, a single dose which is expected to cause a biological effect on 50% of a group of test animals.

Ecologically sustainable use: Ecologically sustainable use of natural resources means use of the natural resources within their capability to sustain natural processes while maintaining the life support systems of nature and ensuring the benefit of the use to the present generation does not diminish the potential to meet the needs and aspirations of future generations.

Ecoregion: An area of similar climate, landform, soil, potential natural vegetation, hydrology, or other ecologically relevant variables.

E coli: Escherichia coli, a bacterium found in the alimentary tract of man and animals.

Ecosystem: A community of organisms considered together with the nonliving factors of its environment.

EF: Environmental Flow

Effective grain size D_{10}: The grain size diameter of a sample such that 10% of the sample is finer.

Effective porosity: That part of the porosity which allows fluid flow.

Effective rainfall: That portion of total precipitation that is available for uptake by plants.

Effective size: The sieve-size opening that will pass 10% of a representative sample of the filter material.

Effluent: Effluent is treated or untreated liquid, solid or gaseous waste discharged by a process such as through a septic tank and leach drain system.

Effluent Stream: A stream that gains water from ground water flow. These streams are typical of humid climates where water tables are high. The discharge of an effluent stream can be sustained by ground water flow for long periods of time between runoff-producing rainfall or snowmelt. Effluent streams generally increase in discharge downstream and contain water throughout the year. The opposite is an influent stream.

EIS: Environmental Impact Statement

Elastic Limit: The maximum stress that can be applied to a body without resulting in permanent deformation - the rock reverts to its original shape after the stress is removed. In the case of a fault or a fold the elastic limit is exceeded and the deformation becomes a permanent structure of the rock.

Electrical conductivity: Conductivity (σ) is an electrical property of water that is used to estimates the volume of TDS or the total volume of dissolved ions in a solution (water), usually corrected to 25°C. Measurement units include milliSiemens per metre and microSiemens per centimetre.

Electro-deionisation (EDI): Production of ultra high purity water using semi permeable membranes and direct current.

Electromagnetic survey (EM): Measurement of the apparent resistivity of the sub-surface by recording the response of a secondary electrical field induced by the pulsing of a current through a fixed or mobile loop.

Electron: A subatomic particle with a negative charge and of negligible mass that orbits the nucleus of an atom

Emergent plants: Erect, rooted, herbaceous plants that may be temporarily or permanently flooded at the base but do not tolerate prolonged inundation of the entire plant.

EMP: Environmental Management Plan

Endangered species: A species that is in imminent danger of becoming extinct.

Endocrine disrupter: Substances that can stop the production or block the transmission of hormones in the body.

Endorheic basin: A closed drainage basin that retains all the water that falls onto it. With no naturally occurring outlet, endorheic basins lose water only through evaporation and infiltration.

Enteric pathogen: Pathogen found in the gut.

Environment: The sum of all conditions and influences affecting the life of organisms.

Environmental allocation: That part of a water resource system that has been set aside for environmental use.

Environmental assets: Include:

Water dependant ecosystems;

Ecosystem services;

Sites with ecological significance

Environmental flow: A water regime provide within a river, wetland or estuary to improve or maintain ecosystems and their benefits where there are competing water uses and where flows are regulated.

Environmental management system: The section of an overall management system that includes structure, planning activities, responsibilities, practices, procurements, processes and resources for developing, implementing, achieving, reviewing and maintaining an environmental an environmental policy.

Environmental manager: An expertise based on function with clearly identified responsibility for the management of environmental water so as to give effect to the environmental objectives of statutory water plans. The institutional form of the environmental manager will vary from place to place reflecting the scale at which the environmental objectives are set and the degree of active management of environmental water required. Also, the environmental manager may be a separate body or an existing Basin, catchment or river manager provided that the function is assigned the necessary powers and resources, potential conflicts of interest are minimised, and the lines of accountability are clear.

Environmental sample: A water sample collected from an aquifer or stream for the purpose of chemical, physical, or biological characterization of the sampled resource.

Environmental service provider: An agency or person undertaking activities directed toward the achievement of environmental objectives.

Environmental setting: Land area characterized by a unique combination of natural and human-related factors, such as row-crop cultivation glacial-till soils.

Environmental tracers: Natural or anthropogenic compounds or isotopes that occur in groundwater, such that their variations or abundances can be used to determine pathways and timescales of environmental processes.

Environmental value: Particular values or uses (sometimes called beneficial uses) of the environment that are important for a healthy ecosystem or for public benefit, welfare, safety or health that require protection from the effects of contaminants, waste discharges and deposits. Several environmental values may be designated for a specific water. Body.

Environmental water provisions: Water allocated to support environmental outcomes and other public benefits. Environmental water provisions recognise the environmental water requirements and are based on environmental, social and economic considerations, including existing user rights.

Environmental water requirements: Descriptions of flow regimes (e.g. volume, timing, seasonality, duration) that are needed to sustain the ecological values of aquatic ecosystems, including their processes and biological diversity, and that are designed to provide environmental outcomes.

Environmentally sustainable level of extraction: The level of water extraction from a particular system which, if exceeded would compromise key environmental assets, or ecosystem functions and the productive base of the resource.

Eolian: A term used in reference to the wind. Eolian materials or structures are deposited by or created by the wind.

Eon: The major divisions of the geologic time scale. Eons are divided into intervals know as "eras". Two eons of the geologic time scale are the Phanerozoic (570 million years ago to present) and the Cryptozoic (4,600 million years ago until 570 million years ago).

EPA: Environmental Protection Authority

Ephemeral stream: A stream or part of a stream that flows only in direct response to precipitation; it receives little or no water from springs, melting snow, or other sources; its channel is at all times above the water table.

Epicenter: The point on the Earth's surface directly above the focus of an earthquake.

Epidemiology: The study of the distribution and determinants of health and disease states in human populations.

Episodic: Composed of a series of episodes.

Epoch: A subdivision of geologic time that is longer than an age but shorter than a period. The Tertiary Period is divided into five epochs. From most recent to oldest they are: Pliocene, Miocene, Oligocene, Eocene and Paleocene.

Equipotential Line: A line in a two-dimensional groundwater flow field such that the total hydraulic head is the same for all points along the line.

Equipotential Surface: A surface in a three dimensional groundwater flow field such that the total hydraulic head is the same everywhere on the surface.

Era: A subdivision of geologic time that is longer than a period but shorter than an eon. Precambrian, Paleozoic, Mesozoic, and Cenozoic are the eras of the time scale from oldest to youngest.

Erosion: The wearing down or washing away of the soil and land surface by the action of water, wind, or ice.

Escherichia coli: Bacterium found in the gut, used as an indicator of faecal contamination of water.

Esker: A long winding ridge of sorted sands and gravel. Thought to be formed from sediment deposited by a stream flowing within or beneath a glacier.

Estuarine wetlands: Tidal wetlands in low-wave-energy environments where the salinity of the water is greater than 0.5 parts per thousand and is variable owing to evaporation and the mixing of seawater and freshwater; tidal wetlands of coastal rivers and embayments, salty tidal marshes, mangrove swamps, arid tidal flats.

Estuary: Area where the current of a stream meets the ocean and where tidal effects are evident; an arm of the ocean at the lower end of a river.

Eutrophication: The process by which water becomes enriched with plant nutrients, most commonly phosphorus and nitrogen. Degradation of water quality due to enrichment by nutrients such as nitrogen and phosphorus, resulting in excessive algal growth and decay and often low dissolved oxygen in the water.

Evaporation: The conversion of a liquid (water) into a vapour (a gaseous state) usually through the application of heat energy during the hydrologic cycle; the opposite of condensation.

Evaporation ponds: These ponds allow produced water from a coal seam gas operation to evaporate, leaving salt residues. They are banned in some areas, like NSW, as they may pose a risk to the local environment if spillage occurs.

Evaporite minerals (deposits): Minerals or deposits of minerals formed by evaporation of water containing salts. These deposits are common in arid climates.

Evaporite: A class of sedimentary rocks composed primarily of minerals precipitated from a saline solution as a result of extensive or total evaporation of water.

Evapotranspiration - The process by which water is discharged to the atmosphere as a result of evaporation from the soil and surface-water bodies and transpiration by plants.

Exchangeable sodium percentage (ESP): The proportion of sodium adsorbed on soil clay mineral surface, as a percentage of total cation exchange capacity. This is used as a measure of soil sodicity.

Exclusion zone: An area which the public will not be able to enter. This is also known as a safety zone.

Exfoliation: A physical weathering process in which concentric layers of rock are removed from an outcrop.

Exotic species: Plants or animals not native to the area.

Expansive clay (expansive soil): A clay soil that expands when water is added and contracts when it dries out. This volume change when in contact with buildings, roadways, or underground utilities can cause severe damage.

Exploration: The work of identifying areas that may contain viable mineral resources. This work can include surface mapping, remote sensing, exploratory drilling, geophysical testing, geochemical testing and other activities.

Exploratory borehole: A borehole drilled for the specific purpose of obtaining information about the subsurface geology or groundwater.

Synonyms are investigation borehole, exploration borehole or pilot borehole.

Exploratory Drilling: Drilling done to locate mineral deposits in an area where little subsurface data about those minerals is available. Exploratory wells may not have the ability to produce the minerals if they are discovered.

Exposed flexible membrane: An uncovered or exposed geo-membrane lined channel is constructed by simply placing the material on the sub-grade of the channel.

Exposure: Contract of a chemical, physical or biological agent with the outer boundary of an organism. This can occur through inhalation, ingestion or dermal contact.

Exposure assessment: The estimation (qualitative or quantitative) of the magnitude, frequency, duration, route and extent of exposure to ore or more contaminated media.

Extraction rate: The rate in terms of unit volume per unit time that water can be drawn from a surface or groundwater system.

Extrusive: Igneous rocks that crystallize at Earth's surface.

F

Facies: The characteristics of a rock mass that reflect its depositional environment. These characteristics enable the rock mass to be distinguished from rocks deposited in adjacent environments.

Fallow: Crop land, tilled or untilled, allowed to lie idle during the whole or greater part of the growing season.

Faecal bacteria: Microscopic single-celled organisms (primarily faecal coliforms and faecal streptococci) found in the wastes of warm-blooded animals. Their presence in water is used to assess the sanitary quality of water for body-contact recreation or for consumption. Their presence indicates contamination by the wastes of warm-blooded animals and the possible presence of pathogenic (disease producing) organisms.

Faecal coliform: See faecal bacteria.

Fault: A fracture or fracture zone in rock along which movement has occurred.

Faunal Succession: A principle of relative dating that is based upon the observed sequence of organisms in the rock record. The relative age of two rock units can frequently be determined by matching the fossils found in those rocks to their positions in the rock record.

Feasible: The benefits outweigh the costs – having considered a number of factors including the environment, economic and social issues.

Felsic: A term used to describe an igneous rock that has a large percentage of light-coloured minerals such as quartz, feldspar, and muscovite. Also used in reference to the magmas from which these rocks crystallize. Felsic rocks are generally rich in silicon and aluminum and contain only small amounts of magnesium and iron. Granite and rhyolite are examples of felsic rocks.

Fen: Peat-accumulating wetland that generally receives water from surface runoff and (or) seepage from mineral soils in addition to direct precipitation; generally alkaline; or slightly acid.

Fertilizer: Any of a large number of natural or synthetic materials, including manure and nitrogen, phosphorus, and potassium compounds, spread on or worked into soil to increase its fertility.

FESWMS: Finite Element Surface Water Modelling System. A 2-D hydrodynamic model developed by the Federal Highways Administration (FHWA), USA.

Fidelity: The degree to which a model application resembles, or is designed to resemble, the physical hydrogeological system (Ritchey and Rumbaugh, 1996). The ASTM guides apply a hierarchical classification of three main fidelities in order of increasing fidelity: Screening, Engineering Calculation and Aquifer Simulator. Higher fidelity models have a capability to provide for more complex simulations of hydrogeological process and/or address resource management issues more comprehensively. In this guide, the term complexity is used in preference to fidelity.

Fidelity, Aquifer Simulator: An Aquifer Simulator is a high fidelity representation of the groundwater system, suitable for predicting the response of a system to arbitrary changes in hydrogeological conditions.

Fidelity, Engineering Calculation or Impact Assessment Model: More detailed assessments are possible with an Engineering Calculation approach, which usually requires more data, better understanding, and greater resources for the study.

Fidelity, Screening Model: With limited data availability and status of hydrogeological understanding, and possibly limited budgets, a Screening model could be suitable for preliminary quantitative assessment (rough calculations), or to guide a field programme.

Field capacity: The greatest amount of water that is possible for a soil to hold in its pore spaces afar excess water has drained away.

Field capacity approximation: The equilibrium water content of an undisturbed soil core at a soil suction of 0.01MPa. If only loose or disturbed soil is available, the equilibrium water content at 0.033MPa suction should be used.

Field water requirement: Total volume of water required to meet the combined water requirements for evapotranspiration, leaching and distribution for a given planning area and period.

FIFO: Fly in / fly out

Fill: Material consisting of uncontaminated sand, coarse stone, clay or drill cuttings.

Filter media: Materials such as activated carbon, charcoal, sand and resins used in water filtration.

Filter pack: See Gravel pack.

Filtering: The soil's ability to attenuate substances by retaining chemicals or dissolved substances on the soil particle surface, transforming chemicals through microbial biological processing, retarding movement, and capturing solid particles.

Filtrate: Liquid that has been passed through a filter.

Filtration: Process in which particulate matter in water is removed by passage through porous media.

Filtration properties: Ability of the drilling fluid to form a controlled filter cake on the wall of the hole under virtually static conditions.

Finite-difference model: A particular kind of numerical model based upon a rectangular grid that sets the boundaries of the model and the nodes where the model will be solved.

Finite-element model: A particular kind of numerical model where the aquifer is divided into a mesh formed of a number of polygonal (usually triangular) cells.

Fire control: Firefighting, but not maintenance and/or drills.

Fixed crest weir: Permanent weir structure across a channel waterway used to measure water flow and/or control upstream water level. This may include both sharp crested and broad crested weirs.

Fjord: A deep, narrow, steep-walled, U-shaped valley that was carved by a glacier and is now occupied by the sea.

Flare: A flame used to burn off unwanted gas; a flare stack is the steel structure on a processing facility from which gas is flared.

Flexible membrane (geomembranes or flexible synthetic liners): A geomembrane is a thin flexible impermeable liner, which combined with the strength of the base soil, can be used to reduce seepage. There are two distinct ways of contrasting channels using geomembranes: covered and exposed flexible membranes.

FLO2DH: See FST2DH.

Flocculation: Process in which small particles are agglomerated into larger particles (which can settle more easily) through gentle stirring by hydraulic or mechanical means.

Flood: Any relatively high streamfiow that overflows the natural or artificial banks of a stream.

Flood attenuation: A weakening or reduction in the force or intensity of a flood.

Flood basalt: A sequence of parallel to subparallel basalt flows that were formed during a geologically brief interval of time and which covered an extensive geographic area. Thought to have formed from simultaneous or successive fissure eruptions.

Flood irrigation: The application of irrigation water whereby the entire surface of the soil is covered by ponded water.

Flood mitigation volume: A volume of storage that is managed to minimise the risks of downstream flooding and may vary throughout the year.

Flood plain: A strip of relatively flat land bordering a stream channel that is inundated at times of high water.

Flow boundary: Any geologic, geomorphic or hydrologic feature which impedes the normal groundwater flow regime. An impermeable rock mass, such as bedrock; a feature which hinders flow across it, such as a fault; or drawdowns resulting from other pumping bores constitute impermeable boundaries and result in an increase in the rate of drawdown. A surface water body, such as a lake or stream, which intersects the aquifer constitutes a recharge boundary and results in a reduction in the rate of drawdown.

Flow line: The idealized path followed by moving particles of water.

Flow net: The set of intersecting equipotential lines and flowlines representing two-dimensional steady flow through an aquifer.

Flowpath: Any route for groundwater movement, extending from a recharge (intake) zone to a discharge (output) zone such as a shallow stream.

Flow rate: The time required for a volume of groundwater to move between points. Typically groundwater moves very slowly; sometimes as little as inches per year.

Flow routing: The process by which flow rates are reduced through the effects of channel or reservoir storage.

Flowing bore: A bore from which groundwater is discharged at the ground surface without the aid of pumping.

Fluid inclusion: A small amount of fluid (liquid and/or gas) trapped within a rock and which is thought to represent the fluid from which the rock crystallized.

Flume: Open conduit having concrete, metal or timber sides and floor used as a supply channel where topography is not suitable for a conventional earthen channel. Flumes are often raised above natural surface and supported by columns or piers.

Fluvial deposit: A sedimentary deposit consisting of material transported by suspension or laid down by a river or stream.

Fluviolacustrine: Refers to sediment deposition from both streams and lakes.

Flux: The act of flowing; a continuous moving on or passing by, as a flowing stream; constant succession; change.

Focus: A point beneath Earth's surface where the vibrations of an earthquake are thought to have originated. Also known as a hypocenter.

Fold: A bend or flexure in a rock unit or series of rock units that has been caused by crustal movements.

Formation: A bed or deposit composed throughout of substantially the same kind of rock; a lithologic unit. Each different formation is given a name.

Formation pressure (Head): Energy contained in a water mass, produced by elevation, pressure or velocity.

Fossil: Remains, imprints or traces of an ancient organism that have been preserved in the rock record. Bones, shells, casts, tracks and excrement can all become fossils.

Fossil fuel: A carbon-rich rock material or fluid, of organic origin that can be produced and burned as a fuel. Coal, oil and natural gas are examples of fossil fuels.

Fracking/Fraccing: Hydraulic fracturing or 'fracking/fraccing' is a process used to stimulate or fracture underground coal seams to increase the flow of gas and water.

Fractured rocks: Hard and impermeable rocks (such as granite) which have fractures and fissures within them that are able to store and transmit water.

Fractured rock aquifer: These occur in igneous and metamorphosed hard rocks which have been subjected to disturbance, deformation, or weathering, and which allow water to move through joints, bedding plains and faults. Although fractured rock aquifers are found over a wide area, they contain much less available groundwater than surficial and sedimentary aquifers and, due to the difficulty of obtaining high yields, the quantities of water taken from them are relatively low.

FRE: Fibreglass-reinforced epoxy – a composite material composed of glass fibres and epoxy resin.

FRP: Firbreglass-reinforced plastic – a composite used for bore casing or riser pipe that is inert to most naturally occurring substances.

Fresh water: Water with less than 500 parts per million dissolved salts.

Freshwater chronic criteria: The highest concentration of a contaminant that freshwater aquatic organisms can be exposed to for an extended period of time (4 days) without adverse effects. See water-quality criteria.

Friable: Descriptive of a rock or mineral that crumbles naturally or is easily broken, pulverized, or reduced to powder.

FST2DH: 2D hydrodynamic flow model developed by the Federal Highway Administration, USA, formerly called FLO2DH. Also, often referred to as the FESWMS Model.

Fumarole: A vent that emits hot gases, usually associated with past or current magmatic activity below.

Fumigant: A substance or mixture of substances that produces gas, vapour, fume or smoke intended to destroy insects, bacteria, or rodents.

Furrow irrigation: A type of surface irrigation whereby water is applied at the upper (higher) end of a field and flows in furrows to the lower end.

G

GAB: Great Artesian Basin is one of the world's largest natural underground water reservoirs and is Australia's largest groundwater basin, containing around 65 million gigalitres (GL) of water, with an annual water recharge of around 880GL. The GAB underlies more than 1.7 million sq kms, extending beneath parts of Queensland, New South Wales, South Australia and Northern Territory. The GAB has been monitored for more than 100 years to ensure its pressure, water levels and quality is maintained.

Gabbro: A black, coarse-grained intrusive igneous rock that is the compositional equivalent of basalt. Composed of calcium-rich feldspars, pyroxene and possibly olivine, but containing little if any quartz.

GABSI: Great Artesian Basin Sustainability Initiative

Gas-In-Place (GIP): The quantity of gas which is estimated to be contained in a known coal formation of discrete area.

Gas turbine power plant: A power plant in which the prime mover is a gas turbine. A gas turbine typically consists of an axial-flow compressor that fees compressed air into one or more combustion chambers where liquid or gaseous fuel is burned. The resultant hot gases are expanded through the turbine, causing it to rotate. The rotating turbine shaft drives the compressors as well as the generator, producing electricity.

Gauge height: The level of surface water at a particular location as measured on a gauge board installed at that location. The gauge zero is normally tied to a reference such as AHD so that the elevation can be determined.

Gauging station: A facility on a stream, lake, canal, reservoir or other water body where instruments are installed to automatically monitor the water. Measurements such as stage, discharge, water temperature and pH are automatically taken and transmitted to hydrologists via satellite, radio or telephone. Measurements from these stations are useful for a wide variety of flood prediction, water management, recreation and navigation purposes.

Gaining stream: A stream in which groundwater discharge contributes significantly to the flow. The same stream could be both a gaining stream and a losing stream, depending on the conditions.

Gas (gaseous): See vapour.

Gas field: The geographic area that is directly above an underground accumulation of natural gas that is commercially viable.

Gateway Process: An independent, scientific and upfront assessment of how a mining or CSG proposal may affect the agricultural values of the land on which it is proposed to be located. The process considers proposals at a very early stage, before a development application can be lodged. The Gateway Process assessment is undertaken by an independent panel of experts from various fields, such as agricultural science, hydrogeology, mining and petroleum.

GBR: Great Barrier Reef

GDE: Groundwater Dependent Ecosystem.

Geochronology: A study of the time relationships of rock units. Includes methods of both relative and absolute dating.

Geomorphic: Pertaining to the form or general configuration of the Earth or of its surface features.

Geomorphology: The science that treats the general configuration of the Earth's surface; the description of land forms.

Geophysics: A branch of geology that uses physical principles to study properties of the earth.

Geothermal: Relating to the Earth's internal heat; commonly applied to springs or vents discharging hot water or steam.

Geothermal gradient: The progressive increase of temperature with depth into the Earth.

Geyser: A hot spring that intermittently erupts a spray of steam and hot water. Caused by the heating of ground water within a confined opening in hot rock

GHG: Greenhouse gases

Ghyben-Herzberg Principle: An equation that relates the depth of a saltwater interface in a coastal aquifer to the height of the freshwater table above sea level under hydrostatic conditions.

Giardia lamblia: A protozoan frequently round in rivers and lakes. If water containing infectious cysts of *Giardia* is ingested, the protozoan can cause a severe gastrointestinal disease called giardiasis.

Gigalitre: 1,000,000,000 litres = 1,000 Megalitres

GIS: Geographic Information System

GJ: Gigajoule (10^9 joules). There are 1000 GJ in a Terajoule (TJ) and 1000 TJ in a Petajoule (PJ).

Glacial: Of or relating to the presence and activities of ice or glaciers.

Glacial drift: A general term for rock material transported by glaciers or icebergs and deposited directly on land or in the sea.

Glacial lake: A lake that derives its water, or much of its water, from the melting of glacial ice also a lake that occupies a basin produced by glacial erosion.

Glacial outwash: Stratified detritus (chiefly sand and gravel) "washed out" from a glacier by meltwater streams and deposited in front of or beyond the end moraine or the margin of an active glacier.

Glacial rebound: A very gradual uplift of Earth's crust that occurs after the weight of a thick continental ice sheet (which produced subsidence) has melted away.

Glacial striations: Grooves and scratches on a bedrock surface that were produced by the movement of a glacier. The orientation of the striations gives evidence to the direction of glacial movement.

Glacial valley: A valley with a U-shaped cross section that was cut by an alpine glacier.

Glacier: A thick mass of ice that forms on land from an accumulation and recrystallization of snow significant enough to persist through the summer and grow year by year. There are two basic types of glaciers: 1) valley (or alpine) glaciers that creep downslope under the influence of gravity, and 2) continental glaciers that flow outward from a thick central area under their own weight.

Glass: An amorphous (without crystal structure) igneous rock that forms from very rapid cooling of magma. The rapid cooling does not provide enough time for crystal growth.

GMS: Groundwater Modelling System.

Gneiss: A coarse-grained, foliated rock produced by regional metamorphism. The mineral grains within gneiss are elongated due to pressure and the rock has a compositional banding due to chemical activity.

Good Industry Practice: The preferred methods that are commonly used to achieve acceptable results. They are used extensively by the majority of drilling contractors.

GPR: Ground penetrating Radar – a near-surface geophysical technique that uses radar to image the subsurface.

Grab sample: Single sample collected at a particular time and place that represents the composition of the water only at that time and place.

Granite: A coarse-grained igneous rock.

Graphical User Interface (GUI): A software package to facilitate the data input, flow simulation and results output of groundwater modelling codes, usually based on the Microsoft Windows system.

Gravel: Clastic sedimentary particles of any composition that are over 2 mm in diameter.

Gravel pack: Granular material introduced into the annulus between the borehole and a casing or perforated lining to prevent or control the movement of finer particles from the aquifer into the bore.

Green energy: Energy that has been sourced from environmentally friendly sources, such as hydro, solar and wind. Also referred to as renewable energy.

Greenstone: A low-grade metamorphic rock that frequently contains green minerals such as chlorite, epidote and talc.

Grey water: Wastewater from the hand basin, shower, bath, spa bath, washing machine, laundry tub, kitchen sink and dishwasher. Water from the kitchen is general too high in grease and oil to be reused successfully without significant treatment.

Ground moraine: A blanket of till that is deposited during the retreat of a glacier.

Groundwater: In the broadest sense, all subsurface water; more commonly, that part of the subsurface water in the saturated zone.

Groundwater basin: The sub- surface area from which groundwater drains. The basins could be separated by geologic or hydrologic boundaries.

Groundwater Dependent Ecosystems (GDE): Ecosystems that rely on groundwater for some or all of their water requirements. For the purposes of defining ecosystem dependence, groundwater may be defined as that water in the system that would be unavailable to plants and animals were it to be extracted by pumping.

Groundwater diversion service: A rural water service which enables customers to divert or pump water from a groundwater source at a specified level of service and which confers common obligations on customers. Typically, service provision involves water access, works or site licence administration, metering or measurement and monitoring of diversions on a regular basis. Aspects of water planning and water resource management may also be involved.

Groundwater divide: The boundary between two adjacent groundwater basins, which is represented by a high point in the water table.

Groundwater flow model: An application of a mathematical model to represent a site-specific groundwater flow system.

Groundwater flow system: The pathway by which groundwater moves from areas of recharge to areas of discharge.

Groundwater head: See hydraulic head.

Groundwater management unit: A hydraulically connected groundwater system that is defined and recognised by state and territory agencies. This definition allows for management of the groundwater resource at an appropriate scale.

Grout: A fluid mixture of cement and water of a consistency that can be pumped through a pipe, to which other additives (e.g. bentonite) may be added to enhance its properties. Sometimes called cement grout or cement slurry.

Grouting: The operation of placing or pumping a grout into an annular or space or cavity.

Growing season: The frost-free period of the year.

GSSHA: Gridded Surface-Subsurface Hydrologic Analysis.

Guideline: Numerical concentration limit or narrative statement recommended to support and maintain a designated water use.

Guideline value: The concentration or measure of a water quality characteristic that, based on present knowledge, either does not result in any significant risk to the health of the consumer (health- related guideline) or is associated with good quality water (aesthetic guideline value).

GW: Groundwater

H

Habitat: The part of the physical environment in which a plant or animal lives.

Half-life: The time required for one half of a sample material to disintegrate.

Hand-dug well: A large-diameter, usually shallow, water well constructed by manual labour. Synonyms are dug well or open well.

Halite: The mineral name for "rock salt". A chemical sedimentary rock that forms from the evaporation of ocean or saline lake waters. It is rarely found at Earth's surface, except in areas of very arid climate. It is often mined for use in the chemical industry or for use as a winter highway treatment. Some halite is processed for use as a seasoning for food.

Halophytic: Salt tolerant vegetation. Often refers to vegetation in groundwater discharge areas in arid or semi arid areas.

Hanging Valley: A tributary to a U-shaped glacial valley which, instead of entering the valley at the same level as the main stream, enters at a higher elevation, frequently as a waterfall. These different stream levels are a result of the rapid down-cutting of the glacier being much faster than the slower down-cutting of the tributary stream.

Hardness: A property of water that causes the formation of an insoluble residue when the water is used with soap and a scale in vessels in which water has been allowed to evaporate. It is due primarily to the presence of ions of calcium and magnesium. Hardness is generally expressed as milligrams per litre as calcium carbonate (CaCO3).

Description	Milligrams per litre as $CaCO_3$
Soft	0-60
Moderately hard	61-120
Hard	121-180
Very hard	more than 180

Hardpan: A relatively hard, impervious, and usually clayey layer of soil lying at or just below land surface; produced as a result of cementation by precipitation of insoluble minerals.

Hazard: A biological, chemical, physical or radiological agent that has the potential to cause harm.

Hazard analysis critical control point (HACCP) system: A systematic methodology to control safety hazards in a process by applying a two-part technique: First, analysis that identifies hazards and their severity and likelihood of occurrence; and second, identification of critical control points and their monitoring criteria to establish controls that will reduce, prevent or eliminate the identified hazards.

Hazard control: The application or implementation of preventive measure that can be used to control identified hazards.

Hazard identification: The process of recognising that a hazard exists and defining its characteristics.

Hazardous event: An incident or situation that can lead to the presence of a hazard (what can happen and how).

Head: See Formation pressure.

Headwaters: The source and upper part of a stream.

Headworks: An assembly bolted to the production casing to control the well, to provide access and protection (e.g. from flooding or vandalism).

Health guideline value: The concentration or measure of a water quality characteristic that, based on current knowledge, does not result in any significant risk to the health of the consumer over a lifetime of consumption (NHMRC & NRMMC 2004a).

Heat Flow: The movement of heat energy from the core of the Earth towards the surface.

Heavy metals: Metallic elements with high atomic weights, (e.g. mercury, chromium, cadmium, arsenic and lead). They can cause damage to living organisms at very low concentrations and tend to accumulate in the food chain.

HEC-HMS: Hydrologic Engineering Centre Hydrologic Modelling System.

HEC-RAS: Hydrologic Engineering Centre River Analysis System.

Helminth: A worm like invertebrate of the order Helminthes. A parasite of humans and other animals.

Hematite: An iron oxide mineral that is commonly used as an ore of iron.

Herbicide: A type of pesticide designed to kill plants.

Heterogeneous: A medium which consists of different (non-uniform) characteristics in different locations.

High recovery: A system which enables a high percentage of water that enters the process to finish up as treated water. Sometimes this can be greater than 90% of process water.

Homogeneous: A medium with identical (uniform) characteristics regardless of location.

Hortonian flow: Overland flow when rainfall exceeds infiltration, can be caused when the water table has risen to ground surface.

Humus: The dark portion of a soil that consists of organic material that is well enough decayed that the original source material cannot be identified.

Hydraulic conductivity (K): The capacity of a rock to transmit water. It is expressed as the volume of water at the existing kinematic viscosity that will move in unit time under a unit hydraulic gradient through a unit area measured at right angles to the direction of flow. It is a property of both the soil matrix and the water passing through it.

Hydraulic Diffusivity: A property of an aquifer or confining bed defined as the ratio of the transmissivity to the storativity.

Hydraulic fracturing: Hydraulic fracturing is a method of extracting natural gas from coal seams. The method has been used in Australia for about 50 years. Sand and fluid are injected from a gas well into the naturally occurring cracks in the coal seam. The same remains in the cracks to prop them open to improve gas flow into the well.

Hydraulic gradient: The change of hydraulic head per unit of distance in a given direction.

Hydraulic head: The height of the free surface of a body of water (e.g. the water surface in a bore), above a given point beneath the surface. For any given point in an aquifer the hydraulic head is the sum of the elevation head (height of the point above a reference datum such as AHD), the pressure head (the column of water above that point) and the velocity head.

Hydraulic resistance (c): The hydraulic resistance is a property of the confining layer of a semi-confined aquifer. It is the resistance against vertical flow and is defined as:

$$c = b'/K'$$

where:

b' = the saturated thickness of the semi-pervious layer.

K' = the hydraulic conductivity of the semi-pervious layer for vertical flow.

If Darcy's law is applied to the confining layer then the hydraulic resistance may be thought of as the drawdown in the aquifer required to produce a unit discharge per unit area from the confining layer.

If $c = \infty$, the aquifer is confined.

Hydraulic resistance has dimensions of Time. The units used are days.

Hydraulics: The science that deals with the laws governing water or other liquids in motion and their applications in engineering.

Hydric soil: Soil that is wet long enough to periodically produce anaerobic conditions, thereby influencing the growth of plants.

Water Resources: Glossary of Terms

Hydrocarbons: A class of compounds containing only hydrogen and carbon, such as methane, ethylene, acetylene and benzene. Fossil fuels such as oil, petroleum and natural gas all contain hydrocarbons.

Hydro-electric: Relating to the generation and distribution of electric energy derived from the energy of falling water or other hydraulic source.

Hydrogeologic properties: The properties of formations that control the movement and storage of groundwater (e.g. hydraulic conductivity, storativity, transmissivity and permeability).

Hydrogeology: The study of the interrelationships of geologic materials and processes with water, especially groundwater.

Hydrograph: Graph showing variation of water elevation, velocity, streamflow, water quality or other property of water with respect to time.

Hydrologic conditions: A set of groundwater inflows, outflows, boundary conditions and hydraulic properties that causes potentiometric heads to adopt a distinct pattern.

Hydrologic cycle (also known as the water cycle): The continuous circulation of water in the Earth-atmosphere system. It describes the path water takes through its various states--vapour, liquid, solid--as it moves from the oceans through the atmosphere, over the land surface as streams, etc or through the groundwater system and back to the oceans.

Hydrologic equation: An expression of the law of mass conservation for purposes of water budgets. It may be stated as inflow equals outflow plus or minus changes in storage.

Hydrologic regime: The characteristic behaviour and total quantity of water involved in a drainage basin.

Hydrologic soil group: A soil characteristic developed by the US National Resource Conservation Service (NRCS) that describes the runoff potential of different soil types using four main soil categories: A, B, C and D.

Hydrology: The study of the occurrence, distribution, and chemistry of all waters of the earth.

Hydrolysis: A chemical reaction involving water that results in the breakdown of mineral material.

Hydrophobic: Not capable of uniting with or absorbing water.

Hydrophyte: Any plant growing in water or on a substrate that is at least periodically deficient in oxygen as a result of excessive water content.

Hydrostatic pressure: The pressure exerted by the water at any given point in a body of water at rest.

Hydrothermal: Pertaining to hot water, the actions of hot water or the products produced by the actions of hot water.

Hydrothermal Deposits: Mineral deposits that are formed by the actions of hot water or gases associated with a magmatic source.

Hydrothermal Metamorphism: Alteration of rock by hot waters or gases associated with a magmatic source.

Hydrothermal Vein: A deposit of minerals precipitated in a fracture by the actions of hot water or gases associated with a magmatic source.

Hypocenter: A point beneath earth's surface where the vibrations of an earthquake are thought to have originated. Also known as the focus.

I

IFD Curve: Intensity-Frequency-Duration Curve (for rainfall).

Igneous rocks: Rocks that have solidified from molten or partly molten material.

Ignimbrite: An igneous rock formed by the lithification of ash flow or pyroclastic flow deposits.

Immobilize: To hold by a strong chemical attraction.

Impact: Has an effect on endpoints, such as people, plants, soil, biota, water or a part of the environment.

Impermeable layer: A layer of material (such as clay) in an aquifer through which water does not pass.

Impermeability: The incapacity of a rock to transmit a fluid.

Impervious: Impermeable. See Impermeability.

Indicator: Measurement parameter or combination of parameters that can be used to assess the quality of water; a specific contaminant, group of contaminants or constituent that signals the presence of something else (e.g. *Escherichia coli* indicate the presence of pathogenic bacteria).

Indicator organisms: Microorganisms whose presence is indicative of pollution or of more harmful microorganisms.

Indirect drinking (potable) reuse: The discharge of recycled water directly into groundwater or surface water with the intent of augmenting drinking water supplies.

Induced recharge: The recharge to an aquifer that occurs when a pumping bore/well creates a cone of depression that lowers an adjacent water table below the level of a stream or lake, causing the stream or lake to contribute water to the aquifer.

Indurated: Cemented, hardened, or a rocklike condition.

Industrial wastewater: Water used by industry in wide-ranging applications generally related to production.

Industrial withdrawals: Water withdrawn for use by industry. The water may be obtained from a public supplier or may be self-supplied.

Infiltration: Flow of water from the land surface into the subsurface.

Infiltration capacity: The maximum rate at which infiltration can occur under specific conditions of soil moisture. For a given soil, the infiltration capacity is a function of the water content.

Infiltration gallery: A shallow horizontal well usually constructed in the bed of a river or along a river bank in an alluvial aquifer.

Infiltration rate: The quantity of water that enters the soil surface in a specified time interval. Often expressed in volume of water per unit of soil surface area per unit of time.

Inflows: Surface water runoff and deep drainage to groundwater (groundwater recharge) and transfers into the water system, (both surface and groundwater), for a defined area.

Infrared: The band of wavelengths within the electromagnetic spectrum between red light of the visible band at 0.7μm and microwaves at 1000 μm. Most remote sensing techniques for channel seepage detection are based on the differences in the infrared reflection/absorption properties of moist and dry soils, and between healthy and stressed vegetation.

Injection well: A well constructed for the purpose of injecting treated water, often wastewater, directly into the ground. Water is generally forced (pumped) into the well for dispersal or storage into a designated aquifer. Injection wells are generally drilled into aquifers that are not used as a drinking water source, unused aquifers, or below freshwater levels.

Inorganic: Containing no carbon; matter other than plant or animal.

Inorganic soil: Soil with less than 20 percent organic matter in the upper 40cm.

Insecticide: A substance or mixture of substance intended to repel insects.

Insignificant: Not valuable or large enough to be considered important.

In-situ field capacity: The percentage of water remaining in a soil two or three days after having been saturated, with the soil surface covered to prevent evapotranspiration and after free drainage has practically ceased.

Instantaneous discharge: The volume of water that passes a point at a particular instant of time.

Instream use: Water use taking place within the stream channel for such purposes as hydroelectric power generation, navigation, water-quality improvement, fish propagation, and recreation. Sometimes called "non-withdrawal use" or "in-channel use".

Integrated catchment management: The coordinated planning, use and management of water, land, vegetation and other natural resources on a river or groundwater catchment, based on cooperation between community groups and government agencies to consider all aspects of catchment management.

Integrated drainage: Drainage developed during geomorphic maturity in an arid region, characterized by coalescence of drainage basins as a result of headward erosion in the lower basins or spilling over from the upper basins.

Integrated management: Any combination of physical, technical, administrative, and legal practices relating to surface water and groundwater in a manner designed to increase combined benefits or achieve a more equitable apportionment of benefits from both sources. Also referred to as conjunctive use.

Intentional discharge: Release of water directly into water bodies for environmental allocation. For example: system maintenance, pressure release, flushing and cleaning of systems, fire drills and equipment maintenance.

Interface: In hydrology, the contact zone between two fluids of different chemical or physical makeup.

Interflow: Water that travels laterally or horizontally through the aeration zone during or immediately after a precipitation event and discharges into a stream or other body of water.

Intergranular pressure: The pressure at the points of contact of grains in a porous medium.

Intermittent stream, see ephemeral stream: A stream that flows only when it receives water from rainfall runoff or springs, or from some surface source such as melting snow.

Interior Drainage: A system of streams that flow into a landlocked basin and evaporate.

Intermediate rock: An igneous rock that has an intermediate silica content. Examples are syenite and diorite. Also see entries for acidic, basic and ultrabasic rocks.

Intermittent stream: A stream that goes dry at certain times of the year. Intermittent streams flow during seasons of the year when runoff and/or groundwater contributions sustain the flow of the stream. They stop flowing during dry seasons when precipitation is low and the water table drops below the bed of the stream.

Internal drainage: Surface drainage whereby the water does not reach the ocean, such as drainage toward the lowermost or central part of an interior basin or closed depression.

Interstices: Voids between grains of sediment.

Intertidal: Alternately flooded and exposed by tides.

Intolerant organisms: Organisms that are not adaptable to human alterations to the environment and thus decline in numbers where alterations occur. See also Tolerant species.

Intrinsic permeability: A measure of the relative ease with which a porous medium can transmit a fluid under a potential gradient and is a property of the medium alone. It is the property of a porous medium itself that expresses the ease with which gases, liquids or other substances can pass through it.

Intrusion: A igneous rock body that formed from magma that forced its way into, through or between subsurface rock units.

Intrusive: Igneous rocks that crystallize below Earth's surface.

Invertebrate: An animal having no backbone or spinal column. See also Benthic invertebrate.

Ion: A positively or negatively charged atom or group of atoms.

Ionic bond: A chemical bond formed by the electrostatic attraction between oppositely charged ions.

Ion exchange: Ion exchange or ion demineralisation is a demineralisation process using high pressure vessels which make use of resin for absorption of salts and minerals in the production of ultra high purity water.

Iron formation: A layered deposit of chemical sedimentary rocks containing at least 15 percent (by weight) iron in the form of sulphide, oxide, hydroxide, or carbonate minerals.

Iron ore: A chemical sedimentary rock that forms when iron and oxygen (and sometimes other substances) combine in solution and deposit as a sediment. Hematite is the most common sedimentary iron ore mineral.

Irrigate: To supply land with water and thereby promote vegetation by means of canals, especially artificially made, passing through it.

Irrigation: The controlled application of water to cropland, hay fields, and/or pasture to supplement that supplied by nature.

Irrigation diversions: The volume of water extracted from waterways for irrigation purposes. The volume includes all losses incurred from when the water is diverted from the river or reservoir until it is delivered to the farm gate.

Irrigation return flow: The part of irrigation applied to the surface that is not consumed by evapotranspiration or uptake by plants and that migrates to an aquifer or surface-water body.

Irrigation withdrawals: Withdrawals of water for application on land to assist in the growing of crops and pastures or to maintain recreational lands.

ISO 9001:2000 (Quality Management): An international accredited standard that provides a generic framework for quality management systems. Designed to assure conformance to specified requirements by a supplier at all stages during the design, development, production, installation and servicing of a product. It sets out the requirements needed to achieve an organisation's aims with respect to guaranteeing a consistent end product.

Isograd: A line on a map that represents a specific degree of metamorphism. Rocks on one side of the line have been subjected to a greater level of metamorphism and on the other side of the line a lower level of metamorphism.

Isostasy: A condition of gravitational balance (similar to floating) in which a mass of lighter crustal rocks are buoyantly supported from below by denser mantle rocks. The crustal rocks above subside into the mantle until they have displaced an adequate amount of mantle material to support them.

Isotope: One of several forms of element. These different forms have the same number of protons but varying number of neutrons.

Isotropic: Having the same properties in all directions.

Isotropy: The condition in which hydraulic properties of the aquifer are equal in all directions.

J

Jade: A translucent gemstone consisting of either jadeite or nephrite that is typically green in colour. Jade is a very durable stone and is used for a variety of jewelry and ornamental objects. Typically cut in the cabochon shape or carved.

Jadeite: A high pressure clinopyroxene that is frequently carved and polished as a gemstone.

Jasper: A variety of coloured chert, typically red or green and often found in association with iron ores. Jasper is frequently used as a gemstone or in the production of ornaments.

Jet: A variety of coal that is frequently cut and polished for jewellery or ornaments.

Jetty: A human made structure built at right angles to a coastline and extending into the water. Jetties are built to protect an area of shoreline from the effects of currents, erosion or deposition.

Joint: A fracture in rock along which there has been no displacement.

Joint set: A group of joints that are parallel or nearly parallel. They are frequently formed at the same time interval from a common process.

Jolly balance: A spring balance used in the determination of specific gravity.

Juvenile water: Water that is new to the hydrologic cycle. Brought to Earth's surface through volcanic eruptions.

K

Karst: A type of topography that results from dissolution and collapse of carbonate rocks such as limestone, dolomite, and gypsum, and that is characterized by closed depressions or sinkholes, caves, and underground drainage.

Kerogen: Solid organic substances frequently found in shales. The organic component of an oil shale.

Kettle: A steep-sided hole or depression, commonly without surface drainage, formed by the melting of a large detached block of stagnant ice that had been buried in the glacial drift.

Kettle lake: A body of water occupying a kettle, as in a pitted outwash plain or in a kettle moraine.

K-feldspar: A potassium feldspar such as orthoclase, microcline, sanidine or adularia. Also referred to as potash feldspar.

Kill: Dutch term for stream or creek.

Kilobar: A unit of pressure equal to 1000 bars (the mean atmospheric pressure at 100 meters above sea level is one bar).

Kilolitre: 1,000 litres.

Kimberlite: A variety of peridotite that is found in volcanic pipes which are thought to be intrusions from the upper mantle. Many diamond deposits are found in kimberlite pipes.

Knickpoint: An abrupt change in slope. A point on a stream profile where a change in gradient occurs. This could be caused by a change in underlying bedrock or bedrock structure.

Knob: A small hilltop that is round in shape.

kPa or Kilopascal: One Kilopascal equals 1000 Pascals (Pa) or 1 KPa = 0.145 lbf/in2

Water Resources: Glossary of Terms

L

Laccolith: An igneous intrusion that has been forced between two layered rock units. The top of the intrusion is arched upwards and the bottom of the intrusion is nearly flat.

Lacustrine: Pertaining to, produced by, or formed in a lake.

Lacustrine wetlands: Wetlands within a lake or reservoir greater than 8 hectares or within a lake or reservoir less than 8 hectares if the water is greater than 2 metres deep in the deepest part of the basin; ocean-derived salinity is less than 500 parts per million.

Lag time (1): The time interval between the centre of mass of rainfall excess (runoff) and the peak discharge at a watershed outlet.

Lag time (2): The lag between a rainfall event and the recharge response being measured at the water table (where depth to water table is many 10s of metres, such as in the Mallee)

Lagoon: A shallow stretch of seawater (or lake water) near or communicating with the sea (or lake) and partly or completely separated from it by a low, narrow, elongate strip of land.

Lahar: A mudflow composed of water and volcanic ash. Lahars can be triggered by the flash melting of the snow cap of a volcanic mountain or from heavy rain. Lahars are very dangerous because they can occur suddenly and travel at great speeds.

Lake: A body of water (fresh or salt) of considerable size, surrounded by land.

Laminar flow: Fluid flow in which the fluid particles move in parallel paths or streamlines. The viscosity of the fluid is dominant and suppresses any tendency towards turbulence.

Land use: A land characteristic that describes the purpose for which land is used, usually with a numerical identifier and a written category.

Landslide: A down-slope movement of rock and soil over a failure surface and under the influence of gravity. Slumps, earthflows, debris flows and debris slides are examples.

Lapilli: Volcanic rock materials which are formed when magma is ejected by a volcano. Typically used for material that ranges between 2 and 64 millimetres in diameter.

Latent heat: The amount of heat given up or absorbed when a substance changes from one state to another, such as from a liquid to a solid.

Lateral moraine: A low ridgelike moraine carried on, or deposited near, the side margin of a mountain glacier.

Lava: Molten rock material on Earth's surface.

Lava Tube: A tunnel below the surface of a solidified lava flow, formed when the exterior portions of the flow solidify and the molten internal material is drained away.

Leaching / leachate: The process by which materials such as organic matter and mineral salts are washed out of a layer of soil or dumped material by being dissolved or suspended in percolating rainwater. The material washed out is known as leachate. Leachate can pollute groundwater and waterways.

Leaching fraction: The fraction of infiltrated irrigation water that percolates below the plant root zone. For this unit to be meaningful, it needs to specify the time over with the leaching fraction is measured and the depth interval over which it is calculated.

Leakance: Controls vertical flow in a model between cells in adjacent layers. Equivalent to effective vertical hydraulic conductivity divided by the vertical distance between layer midpoints.

Leakage coefficient: The leakage coefficient is a property of the confining layer of the semi-confined aquifer. It is the inverse of hydraulic resistance and is defined as:

Leakage Coefficient = K'/b'

where:

K' = hydraulic conductivity of the semi-pervious layer for vertical flow.

b' = saturated thickness of the semi-pervious layer.

Leakage coefficient may be defined as the rate at which water will leak from a unit area of the confining layer per unit drawdown in the aquifer proper.

It has the dimensions of 1/time. The units of leakage coefficient are day $^{-1}$.

Leakage Factor: The leakage factor is a property of the semi-confined aquifer.

It is defined as:

$$L = \sqrt{(Kbc)}$$

where:

c = hydraulic resistance of the semi-pervious layer.

K = hydraulic conductivity of the aquifer material.

b = thickness of the aquifer.

The leakage factor describes the distribution of leakage into a semi-confined aquifer. High values of L indicate that the influence of leakage will be small, i.e. a high resistance of the semi-pervious layer to flow, as compared with the resistance of the aquifer itself.

The dimensions of L are in length. The units of L are metres.

Leaky aquifer: A leaky or semi-confined aquifer is a pressure aquifer for which the confining layers are not completely impervious. The hydraulic conductivity of the confining layer may be very small when compared with that of the aquifer material, but as the radius of influence of a discharging facility increases, the area through which the confining layer is contributing water becomes very large and the volume of water contributed can be a very significant part of the total water discharged. The flow of water from the confining layer to the aquifer is assumed to be vertical. The horizontal movement in this layer is negligible.

Leaky confining layer: A low-permeability layer that can transmit water at sufficient rates to furnish some recharge to a well pumping from an under-lying aquifer. Also known as an aquitard.

Left bank, right bank: Left and right sides of a channel or drain when looking in the direction of the flow.

Lethal concentration, 50% (LC50): The atmospheric concentration found to be lethal to 50% of a group of test animals exposed for the specified time.

Lethal dose, 50% (LD50): The does found to be lethal in 50% of a group of test animals when administered by the specified route, e.g. oral or dermal.

Levee: A long continuous ridge built by people along the banks of a stream to contain the water during times of high flow. Natural levees can also be built along the banks of a stream. When the flood water decelerates upon leaving the channel, sediments quickly drop out of suspension and build a ridge over time.

Limestone: A sedimentary rock consisting chiefly of calcium carbonate, primarily in the form of the mineral calcite.

Lineament: A regional topographic feature of regional extent that is believed to reflect crustal structure.

Liner: A casing, screen or other device inserted into a larger casing, screen or open hole as a means of sealing off undesirable material or maintaining the structural integrity of the well.

Liquefied Natural Gas (LNG): Natural gas that has been converted to the liquid state by reducing its temperature. (At standard surface temperature and pressure the liquification temperature is about -260 degrees Fahrenheit.)

Liquid: The part of the hydrologic cycle in which molecules move freely among themselves but do not separate like those in a vapour/gaseous state.

Liquefaction: Refers to the process by which water-saturated, unconsolidated sediments are transformed into a substance that acts like a liquid, often in an earthquake.

Lithification: The processes through which sediments are converted into sedimentary rock, including compaction and cementation.

Lithology: The study and description of rocks, including their mineral composition and texture. Also used in reference to the compositional and <u>textural</u> characteristics of a rock.

Lithosphere: The rigid outer shell of the earth which includes the crust and a portion of the upper mantle.

Lithospheric plate: A large slab of the lithosphere that can be moved by convection current motion within the mantle.

LNAPL (Light Non-Aqueous Phase Liquid): An LNAPL is one of a group of organic substances that are relatively insoluble in water and are less dense than water. LNAPLs, such as oil, tend to spread across the surface of the water table and form a layer on top of the water table."

LNG: Liquefied natural gas is an odour4less, colourless, non-corrosive and non-toxic natural gas production consisting primarily of methane (CH4). It is in liquid form at near atmospheric pressure.

LNG train: The refrigeration unit which cools natural gas to a liquid. There are four main elements in the cooling cycle: Impurity removal, dehydration, compression and liquefaction using heat exchangers.

Load: Material that is moved or carried by streams. It is reported as weight of material transported during a specified time period, such as tonnes per year.

Local groundwater system: Aquifers which respond rapidly to recharge due to a shallow watertable and/or close proximity of the recharge and discharge sites. These types of flow systems occur almost exclusively in unconfined aquifers.

Lode: A rich accumulation of minerals in solid rock. Frequently in the form of a vein, layer or an area with a large concentration of disseminated particles.

Loess : A widespread homogeneous commonly non-stratified porous, friable, slightly coherent, fine grained blanket deposit of wind-blown and wind deposited silt and fine sand.

Log removal: Used in reference to the physical-chemical treatment of water to remove, kill or inactivate microorganisms such as bacteria, protozoa and viruses (1-log removal = 90% reduction in density of the targeted organism, 2-log removal = 99% reduction, 3-log removal = 99.9% reduction, etc.).

Long-term monitoring: The collection of data over a period of many years to assess changes in selected hydrologic conditions.

Longitudinal dune: A long, narrow sand dune that has its long dimension oriented parallel to the direction of the wind.

Longitudinal profile: A cross section of a stream or valley beginning at the source and continuing to the mouth. These profiles are drawn to illustrate the gradient of the stream.

Longshore current: A flow of water parallel to a coastline that is caused by waves striking the coast at an oblique angle.

Longshore drift: The movement of sediment along a coastline caused by waves striking the coast at an oblique angle. The waves wash sediment particles up the beach at an oblique angle and the swash back to the sea carries the particles down the gradient of the beach. This produces a zig-zag path of particle movement along the beach.

Losing stream: A stream that is losing water to (or recharging) the groundwater system. The same stream could be both a gaining stream and a losing stream, depending on the conditions.

Loss of biodiversity: Mortality of native biota resulting in reduced ecosystems, species or genetic diversity.

Lowland: A relatively flat area in the lower levels of regional elevation.

LPG: Liquid Petroleum Gas.

Lumped parameter model: A type of numerical model that averages input parameters into a single value across the modelling domain. Lumped parameter models are best suited for areas with mostly homogenous properties.

Luster: The manner in which light reflects from a mineral surface. Metallic, submetallic and non-metallic are the basic types of luster.

Lysimeter: A field device containing a soil column and vegetation; used for measuring evapotranspiration.

M

Macrophyte: A member of the macroscopic plant life of an area, especially of a body of water; large aquatic plant.

Mafic: A term used to describe an igneous rock that has a large percentage of dark-coloured minerals such as amphibole, pyroxene and olivine. Also used in reference to the magmas from which these rocks crystallize. Mafic rocks are generally rich in iron and magnesium. Basalt and gabbro are examples of mafic rocks.

Magma: Molten rock material that occurs below Earth's surface.

Magma chamber: A full or emptied magma reservoir in the shallow portion of the lithosphere.

Magmatic water: Water that is dissolved in a magma or water that is released from a magma. Some magmas can contain up to several percent dissolved water by weight.

Magnetic anomaly: An increase or decrease in the local magnetic field compared to the normally expected value.

Magnetic declination: The horizontal angular difference between True North and Magnetic North.

Magnetic inclination: The vertical angular difference between a horizontal plane and the orientation of Earth's magnetic field.

Magnetic north: The direction that a compass points. The location where Earth's magnetic field dips vertically into the Earth.

Magnetic reversal: A change in the polarity of Earth's magnetic field in which the north magnetic pole becomes the south magnetic pole and vice versa. Also known as geomagnetic reversal or polarity reversal. Earth's magnetic field has reversed many times in the past and the time intervals between these changes are known as polarity epochs.

Magnetic stratigraphy: The correlation of rock units and study of Earth's history using magnetic events and magnetic epochs as a time reference.

Magnetometer: An instrument designed to measure the strength and character of Earth's magnetic field.

Magnitude: A measure of earthquake strength based upon the amount of ground motion experienced and corrected for the distance between the observation point and the epicentre. There are several magnitude scales in use.

Main stem: The principal trunk of a river or a stream.

Major extracted water storages: Major off-river storages that primarily store water extracted from rivers or aquifers, or from flood water emanating from rivers.

Major impact: Potentially lethal to the local ecosystem.

Major ions: Constituents commonly present in water in concentrations exceeding 1.0 milligram per litre. Major cations are calcium, magnesium, sodium, and potassium. The major anions are sulphate, chloride, fluoride, nitrate, and those contributing to alkalinity (see alkaline), most generally assumed to be bicarbonate and carbonate.

Major on-stream storages: Major storages on defined watercourses.

Major storages: Storages greater than 1,000 megalitres in volume are considered to be major storages.

Make good: If water extraction by a CSG operation is affecting an existing bore, then the relevant CSG company must undertake restoration measures to restore the bore's capacity to supply water or provide the bore owner with an alternative water supply. The bore owner and CSG company may also agree to a monetary settlement.

Manganese nodule: A rounded concretion, rich in manganese minerals with minor concentrations of cobalt, copper and nickel. These occur in abundance on some parts of the deep ocean floor and have been considered as a potential source of manganese.

Manning's equation: An equation that can be used to compute the average velocity of flow in an open channel.

Mantle: A major subdivision of Earth's internal structure. Located between the base of the crust and overlying the core.

Mantle plume: A rising mass of hot mantle material that can create an area of volcanic activity in the centre of a lithospheric plate.

MAR: Managed Aquifer Recharge

Marble: A non-foliated metamorphic rock that is produced from the metamorphism of limestone. It is composed primarily of calcium carbonate

Marine wetland: Wetlands that are exposed to waves and currents of the open ocean and to water having a salinity greater than 30,000 parts per million; present along the coastlines of the open ocean.

Marsh: A water-saturated, poorly drained area, intermittently or permanently water covered, having aquatic and grass-like vegetation.

Massive: A term used in reference to a rock unit that is homogeneous in texture, fabric and appearance.

Mass wasting (also mass movement): A general term used for any downslope movement of rock, soil, snow or ice under the influence of gravity. Includes: landslides, creep, rock falls and avalanches.

Matric potential: A variable describing how strongly the water within a soil matrix is bound to the soil by capillary and other forces.

Maturity: A stage in the evolutionary erosion of land areas in which the flat uplands have been widely dissected by deep river valleys.

Maturity (stream): The stage in the development of a stream at which it has reached its maximum efficiency, when velocity , is just sufficient to carry the sediment to it by tributaries; characterized by a broad, open, flat-floored valley having a moderate gradient and gentle slope.

Maximum allowable depletion: The maximum level of depletion to which the soil can dry without causing water deficit stress in a crop that has a fully expanded root zone. Notationally, the sum of the readily available water in each soil horizon with the plant root zone with an allowance made for the soil water extraction pattern of the crop.

Maximum risk: Risk in the absence of preventative measures.

MCF or Mcf: Thousand cubic feet (10^3 cubic feet)

Mean: The arithmetic average of a set of observations, unless otherwise specified.

Mean discharge (MEAN): The arithmetic mean of individual daily mean discharges of a stream during a specific period, usually daily, monthly, or annually.

Meandering Stream: A stream that has many bends (meanders). This type of drainage pattern usually develops on a nearly level landscape and where the banks of the stream are easily eroded.

Measurement flume: A section of concrete channel flume with specially shaped sidewalls and/or floor that forms a constriction in the waterway. Measurement of the difference in water surface levels through the constriction allows calculation of water flow rate by referral to rating tables calibrated for the site. Particular types of measurement flume include the Parshall and Venturi flumes.

Mechanical Weathering: A general term applied to a variety of weathering processes that result in the particle size reduction of rock materials with no change in composition. Frost action, salt crystal growth and pressure relief fracturing are examples. Also known as physical weathering.

Medial moraine: A streak of till in the centre of a glacier. These are found down-slope from the junction of two glaciers and are a merging of their lateral moraine deposits.

Median: The middle or central value in a distribution of data ranked in order of magnitude. The median is also known as the 50th percentile.

Median effective concentration, 50%: see EC50.

Medical geology: The study of human health related to geology. Examples would include the correlation of disease or vitality with residences over specific types of bedrock or health problems associated with exposure to specific mineral materials.

Megalitre: 1,000,000 litres.

Membrane: A molecular filter used in the separation process of molecules.

Membrane bioreactor: MBR is a microfiltration technology used for the treatment of municipal and industrial wastewater to produce water suitable for discharge into environmental water ways or to be reclaimed for irrigation purposes. It does this by removing suspended solids.

Membrane separation technology: The use of thin barriers (membranes) between miscible fluids for separating a mixture.

Mesophyte: Any plant growing where moisture and aeration conditions lie between the extremes of "wet" and "dry."

Metabolite: A substance produced in or by biological processes.

Metamorphic rocks: Rocks derived from pre-existing rocks by mineralogical, chemical, or structural changes (essentially in a solid state) in response to marked changes in temperature, pressure, shearing stress, and chemical environment at depth in the Earth's crust.

Metamorphism: Alteration of the minerals, textures and composition of a rock caused by exposure to heat, pressure and chemical actions.

Meteoric water: Water from the atmosphere, such as rain, snow, hail, or sleet.

Meteor: A meteoroid that penetrates Earth's atmosphere, producing a streak of bright light caused by incineration.

Meteorite: A particle of iron or rock that has fallen to Earth's surface from inter-planetary space.

Meteoroid: A particle of iron or rock found in inter-planetary space. Distinguished from planets or asteroids by its much smaller size.

Methane (CH_4): Methane is a naturally occurring and odourless gas which is the main component of natural gas in coal seams. It is not toxic and traces of CH_4 are in the air we breathe

Method detection limit: The minimum concentration of a substance that can be accurately identified and measured with current laboratory technologies.

MDB: Murray Darling Basin

MDBA: Murray Darling Basin Authority

Micro-filtration: Removal of particulate within the 0.1 – 1 micron range through the use of a microporous membrane.

Micrograms per litre (µg/L): A unit expressing the concentration of constituents in solution as weight (micrograms) of solute per unit volume (litre) of water; equivalent to one part per billion in most stream water and groundwater. One thousand micrograms per litre equals one milligram per litre.

Microfiltration: The process of passing wastewater through porous membranes in the form of sheets or tubes to remove suspended and particulate material. Pore sizes can be very small and particles down to 0.2 microns can be retained.

Microorganism: Organism too small to be visible to the naked eye. Bacteria, viruses, protozoa and some fungi and algae are microorganisms.

Microseism: A vibration of the Earth that is unrelated to earthquake activity - instead it is caused by wind, moving trees, ocean waves or human activity.

Milligram (mg): A mass equal to 10^{-3} grams.

Milligrams per litre (mg/L): A unit expressing the concentration of chemical constituents in solution as weight (milligrams) of solute per unit volume (litre) of water; equivalent to one part per million in most stream water and groundwater.

Water Resources: Glossary of Terms

Mineral: A naturally occurring, inorganic solid with a definite chemical composition and an ordered internal structure.

Mineral soil: Soil composed predominantly of mineral rather than organic materials; less than 20 percent organic material.

Mineralogy: The study of minerals - their composition, structure, formation, uses, properties, occurrence and geographic distribution.

Minimum reporting level (MRL): The smallest measured concentration of a constituent that may be reliably reported using a given analytical method. In many cases, the MRL is used when documentation for the method detection limit is not available.

Mining: See over withdrawal. The permanent removal from the ground of a substance such as an ore body or the removal of groundwater at a rate greater than is sustainable.

Minor catchment storages: Small storages (farm dams) that are not on defined waterways or watercourses that are not filled from extracted water or flood flows out of rivers but from local catchment runoff.

Minor extracted water storages: Minor off-river storages (e.g. farm dams) that primarily store water extracted from rivers or aquifers, or from flood water emanating from rivers.

Minor impact: Potentially harmful to the local ecosystem.

Minor on-stream storages: Small storages (farm dams) on minor watercourses.

Minor storages: Storages less than 1,000 megalitres in volume are considered to be minor storages for the purposes of the water balance.

Mitigation: Actions taken to avoid, reduce, or compensate for the effects of human-induced environmental damage.

MMbbl: Million barrels

MMboe: Million barrels of oil equivalent

MMbopd: Million barrels of oil per day

MMCF or MMcf: Million cubic feet (10^6 cubic feet)

MMCFD or MMcfd: Million cubic feet per day

Model application: Refer to Model, Groundwater.

Model calibration: The process by which the independent variables (parameters) of a numerical model are adjusted, within realistic limits, to produce the best match between simulated and observed data (usually water-level values). This process involves refining the model representation of the hydrogeologic framework, hydraulic properties, and boundary conditions to achieve the desired degree of correspondence between the model simulations and observations of the groundwater flow system.

Model, Conceptual: A simplified and idealised representation (usually graphical) of the physical hydrogeologic setting and our hydrogeological understanding of the essential flow processes of the system. This includes the identification and description of the geologic and hydrologic framework, media type, hydraulic properties, sources and sinks, and important aquifer flow and surface-groundwater interaction processes.

Model, Groundwater: An application of a mathematical model to represent a site-specific groundwater flow system. A groundwater model provides a scientific means to synthesise the available data into a numerical characterisation of a groundwater system. The model represents the groundwater system to an adequate level of detail, and provides a predictive tool to quantify the effects on the system of specified hydrological stresses.

Model, Mathematical model: A mathematical model is a set of equations, which, subject to certain assumptions, quantifies the physical processes active in the aquifer. While the model itself obviously lacks the detailed reality of the groundwater system, the behaviour of a valid model approximates that of the aquifer.

Model, Analytical model: Refer to Analytical Model

Model, Numerical model: Refer to Numerical Model.

Moderate impact: Potentially harmful to the regional ecosystem.

MODFLOW: Industry standard groundwater flow model developed by the US Geologic Survey (USGS).

Modified soil mix (lime, gypsum, cement, chemicals): To improve the slope stability, erosion resistance and permeability of the soil being used in the channel construction (in-situ or imported), soil may be treated or mixed with relatively small quantities of substances such as lime, cement, gypsum, and certain chemicals to overcome their natural deficiencies.

Mohorovicic discontinuity: The boundary between the crust and the mantle. Frequently referred to as the Moho.

Mohs hardness scale: A collection of minerals ranging from very soft to very hard. Use as a comparison scale during mineral identification. From softest to hardest, the ten minerals are: talc 1, gypsum 2, calcite 3, fluorite 4, apatite 5, orthoclase 6, quartz 7, topaz 8, corundum 9, and diamond 10. Developed by Friedrich Mohs, a German mineralogist in the early 1800's.

Monitoring: Repeated observation, measurement, or sampling at a site, on a scheduled or event basis, for a particular purpose.

Monitoring bore/well: A non-pumping bore/well, generally of small diameter, that is used to monitor groundwater properties such as water quality or water levels. A piezometer, which is open only at the top and bottom of its casing, is one type of monitoring bore.

Monocline: An area of increased dip in otherwise gently dipping strata.

Monocyclic araomatic hydrocarbons: Single-ring aromatic compounds. Constituents of lead-free gasoline; also used in the manufacture of monomers and plasticizers in polymers.

Monte Carlo analysis: A set of model simulations for alternative model realisations, on the assumption that aspects of the model are stochastic. A *realisation* is one of many possible valid descriptions of a model in terms of its aquifer parameters, boundary conditions or stresses.

Moraine: A mound, ridge, or other distinct accumulation of unsorted, unstratified glacial drift, predominantly till, deposited chiefly by direct action of glacier ice.

Most probable number: Most probable number is a measure of microbiological contamination.

MOU: Memorandum of Understanding

Mound springs: These occur in the southwestern and western margins of the Great Artesian Basin. When the water comes to the surface in these arid environments, minerals are precipitated around the spring by evaporative concentration and cooling. The springs are sites of rich endemic flora and fauna. They have long been important to the Aboriginal people and to the pastoral industry.

Mountain: A general term used in reference to an area that is at a conspicuously higher elevation than surrounding lands. Mountains are larger than hills and are significant enough in relief that they are given names by local residents.

Mouth: The place where a stream discharges to a larger stream, a lake, or the sea.

mPa or Megapascal: 10^6 Pascals

MRS (Magnetic Resonance Sounding): Technique is based on NMR principle (Nuclear Magnetic Resonance), a geophysical technique that can directly detect the presence of water.

Mtpa: Million tonnes per annum (of LNG)

Muck: Dark, finely divided, well-decomposed, organic matter forming a surface deposit in some poorly drained areas. Muskeg: - Large expanses of peatlands or bogs in subarctic zones.

Mud cake thickness: See Wall cake thickness.

Mudflow: A type of mass movement composed mainly of clay-size materials with a high enough water content that it flows readily..

Mudstone: A sedimentary rock composed of clay-size particles but lacking the stratified structure that is characteristic of a shale.

Multi-media filtration: Removal of coarse particulate within the 20 – 25 micron range.

Multiple barriers: Use of more than one preventive measure as a barrier against hazards.

Municipal: Belonging to a town, city or district that has its own local government. For municipal use of recycled water, this refer to the town, city or district irrigating race tracks, ovals, lawn bowls greens, roadsides, parklands, golf courses and any other area under their control.

Municipal water system: A network of pipes, pumps, and storage and treatment facilities designed to deliver potable water to homes, schools, businesses, and other users in a city or town and to remove and treat waste materials.

MW or Megawatt: A unit of power

MWh: Megawatt hour – a metric unit of energy, especially electrical energy.

MY: Million years - abbreviation.

MYA.: Million years ago - abbreviation.

Mylonite: A brecciated metamorphic rock frequently found in a fault zone. The fractured texture is thought to form by the crushing actions of fault movement.

N

Naegleria fowleri: An amoeba that causes a form of meningitis.

Nano-filtration: A membrane based process that gives a level of filtration greater than 0.001 microns.

Nannofossils: A generic term used in reference to very small fossils that are at the limit of resolution by a light microscope. They are therefore studied with electron microscopes and are frequently fossil discoasters and coccoliths.

NAPL (Non-Aqueous Phase Liquid): Many contaminants, including chlorinated solvents and petroleum products, enter the subsurface in the form of an oily liquid, known as a NAPL. NAPLs do not mix readily with water and therefore flow separately from ground water. If the NAPL is more dense than water (known as DNAPL), it will tend to sink once it reaches the water table. If the liquid is less dense than water (known as an LNAPL), it will tend to float on the water table."

Nappe: A large slab of earth's surface that has been moved in a horizontal or near horizontal direction over a plane of separation. This motion can be produced by faulting or sliding. The term is generally used for very large slabs which are many square kilometres in surface area.

Native metal: A natural deposit of a metallic element such as gold, silver, copper or iron in a pure form.

Natural bridge: An arch-shaped rock formation produced by weathering and/or erosion.

Natural gas: Naturally occurring <u>hydrocarbons</u> that exist in subsurface rock units in the gaseous state. Methane is the most abundant but ethane, propane and others also occur.

Natural levee: A long, broad, low ridge built by a stream on its flood plain along one or both banks of its channel in time of flood.

Nebula: A cloud of interstellar dust that is faintly visible from Earth.

Nephelometric turbidity units (NTU): A measure of turbidity in water.

Network: Finite element or difference grid or mesh used to divide a numerical modelling domain for hydrologic, hydraulic or groundwater modelling.

Neumann condition: Also called a constant flux boundary. The boundary condition for a groundwater flow model where a flux across the boundary of the flow region is known and specified, and the model computes the associated aquifer head.

Neutron: A subatomic particle, contained in the nucleus of an atom. It has no electrical charge and a mass similar to that of a proton.

Nitrate: An ion consisting of nitrogen and oxygen (NO_3^-). Nitrate is a plant nutrient and is very mobile in soils.

Nitrification: The oxidation of ammonia nitrogen to nitrate nitrogen in wastewater by biological means.

Nitrogen: An important nutrient found in high concentrations in recycled waters, originating from human and domestic wastes. A useful plant nutrient that can also cause off-site problems of eutrophication in lakes, rivers and estuaries. It can also contaminate groundwater.

Nodule: A mineral mass that has a different composition or is more weathering resistant than its surrounding rock. These are normally rounded in shape. Examples include: chert masses in a limestone rock unit, pyrite masses in a coal seam, or carbonate masses in a shale. In most cases these "nodules" have formed within the rock unit or its former sediment mass. The term is also applied to rounded masses of manganese minerals that occur on some parts of the ocean floor.

Nominal diameter: An approximate diameter (internal or external) of the tube, usually used for simple identification purposes. For example, a 100mm diameter tube may vary within a manufacturing range of 99.5mm to 100.5mm.

Noncontact water recreation: Recreational activities, such as fishing or boating, that do not include direct contact with the water.

Non-persistent emergent plants: Emergent plants whose leaves and stems break down at the end of the growing season from decay or by the physical forces of waves and ice; there are at certain times no visible traces of the plants above the surface of the water.

Nonpoint-source contaminant: A substance that pollutes or degrades water that comes from lawn or cropland runoff, the atmosphere, roadways, and other diffuse sources.

Nonpoint-source water pollution: Water contamination that originates from a broad area (such as leaching of agricultural chemicals from crop land) and enters the water resource diffusely over a large area.

Non-renewable groundwater: Groundwater extracted from an aquifer that receives limited or no recharge (i.e. 'mining' of the resource or use of long term aquifer storage).

Non-saline groundwater: Groundwater with a salinity concentration less than 3500 milligrams per litre.

Non-selective herbicide: Kills or significantly retards growth of most higher plant species.

Non-uniqueness: The principle that many different possible sets of model inputs can produce nearly identical computed aquifer head distributions for any given model.

Normal Fault: A fault with vertical movement and an inclined fault plane. The block above the fault has moved down relative to the block below the fault.

Nuclear electric power (nuclear power): The generation of electricity using the heat released from a nuclear fuel.

Nuclear fuel: Fissionable materials that are rich enough to sustain a fission chain reaction.

Nuclear reactor: A facility where a nuclear fission chain reaction can be initiated, controlled, and sustained.

Nuisance species: Undesirable plants and animals, commonly exotic species.

Numerical model: A model of groundwater flow in which the aquifer is described by numerical equations, with specified values for boundary conditions that are usually solved on a digital computer. In this approach, the continuous differential terms in the governing hydraulic flow equation are replaced by finite quantities. The computational power of the computer is used to solve the resulting algebraic equations by matrix arithmetic. In this way, problems with complex geometry, dynamic response effects and spatial and temporal variability may be solved accurately. This approach must be used in cases where the essential aquifer features form a complex system, and where surface-groundwater interaction is an important component (ie. high complexity models).

Nutrient imbalance: Unbalanced supply of plant mineral nutrients resulting in plant deficiencies and toxicities.

Nutrient load: The amount of nutrient reaching the waterway over a given timeframe (usually per year) from its catchment area.

Nutrients: Minerals, particularly inorganic compounds of nitrogen (nitrate and ammonia) and phosphorous (phosphate) dissolved in water which provide nutrition (food) for plant growth.

O

Oblique-slip fault: A fault that has both horizontal and vertical elements of displacement.

Observation bore/well: A bore/well which has been constructed to obtain information on variations in groundwater parameters such as water level or water quality.

Obsidian: A glassy igneous rock with a composition similar to granite. The glassy texture is a result of cooling so fast that mineral lattices were not developed.

Offshore: The geographic area that is seaward of a coastline.

Oil field: The geographic area above an underground accumulation of oil and natural gas.

Oil shale: A dark-colored shale containing an unusual amount of solid organic material known as kerogen. This shale can be crushed and heated to liberate gaseous and liquid hydrocarbons. At present the expenditure required to process oil shale into a fuel makes this effort marginally profitable or unprofitable.

Old age: A stage in the development of a landscape when streams have a low gradient and meander back and forth across broad floodplains. The landscape is marked by meander scars and oxbow lakes.

Oolite: A small sphere of calcium carbonate no more than a few millimetres in diameter and with a concentric internal structure. These spheres are thought to have formed by inorganic precipitation of calcium carbonate in very thin layers around a grain of sand or a particle of shell or coral. A rock composed primarily of oolites.

Oolitic: A limestone texture that is characterized by spherical grains of calcium carbonate with a concentric internal structure. These grains are thought to form by inorganic precipitation of calcium carbonate around a sand grain or shell particle nucleus.

Opaque: An adjective used in reference to a substance that does not allow light of visible wavelength to enter or pass through. Minerals with a metallic or submetallic lustre are normally opaque.

Operational monitoring: The planned sequence of measurements and observations used to assess and confirm that individual barriers and preventive strategies from controlling hazards are functioning properly and effectively.

Ophiolite suite: The typical sequence of rocks in the oceanic crust: from bottom to top: ultrabasic rocks, gabbro, sheeted dikes, pillow basalts, and sea-floor sediments. Igneous rocks and deep-sea sediments associated with divergence zones and the sea-floor environment.

Orbit: An elliptical or hyperbolic path travelled by a satellite object around a more massive body. For example, the Earth orbits the Sun.

Ore deposit: A natural accumulation of a metal, gemstone or other valuable mineral substance, which is rich enough in concentration that it can be mined and processed at a profit.

Ore mineral: A mineral that contains a high enough concentration of a useful element or compound that the element or compound can be extracted at a profit.

Original horizontality: One of the principles of relative dating. Based upon the good assumption that sedimentary rocks are deposited in horizontal or nearly horizontal layers; then if sedimentary layers are found in an inclined orientation the force that moved them to that orientation must have been applied at some time after their deposition.

Orogenic belt: A linear or arcuate region of folded and uplifted rocks.

Orogeny: A compressive tectonic process that results in intense folding, reverse faulting, crustal thickening, uplift and deep plutonic activity. A mountain-building episode.

Oscillation ripple marks: Symmetrical ridges in sand or other sediment that are caused by a back-and-forth wave action.

Organic: Containing carbon, but possibly also containing hydrogen, oxygen, chlorine, nitrogen, and other elements.

Organic detritus: Any loose organic material in streams - such as leaves, bark, or twigs removed and transported by mechanical means, such as disintegration or abrasion.

Organic soil: Soil that contains more than 20 percent organic matter in the upper 40cm.

Organochlorine compound: Synthetic organic compounds containing chlorine. As generally used, the term refers to compounds containing mostly or exclusively carbon, hydrogen, and chlorine. Examples include organochlorine insecticides, polychlorinated biphenyls, and some solvents containing chlorine.

Organonitrogen herbicides: A group of herbicides consisting of a nitrogen ring with associated functional groups and including such classes as triazines and acetanilides. Examples include atrazine, cyanazine, alachlor, and metolachor.

Organophosphate insecticides: A class of insecticides derived from phosphoric acid. They tend to have high acute toxicity to vertebrates. Although readily metabolized by vertebrates, some metabolic products are more toxic than the parent compound.

Orographic: Pertaining to mountains, in regard to their location and distribution; said of the precipitation caused by the lifting of moisture-laden air over mountains.

Osmosis: The natural processes that occurs when water flows spontaneously from a purer solution through a semi-permeable membrane into a more complex solution.

Outcrop: An exposure of bedrock. Outcrops can be formed naturally or by human action. Stream erosion and highway construction can produce outcrops.

Outfall: A location where water is discharged. Normally used in reference to where a water treatment facility releases treated water into the environment.

Outfall structure: Regulating structure located at the downstream end, or intermediate points, of a supply channel to allow safe discharge of surplus flows arising in the system due to the effects of rainfall inflow, planned channel shutdown or operational error. An outfall can also be used to drain water from the channel at the end of the irrigation season. Water released through the outfall is usually discharged to a drainage channel, natural waterway or regulating storage.

Outgassing: The release of juvenile gases and water to the surface from a magma source.

Outwash: Soil material washed down a hillside by rainwater and deposited upon more gently sloping land.

Overland flow: The flow of rainwater or snowmelt over the land surface toward stream channels.

Overwithdrawal: Withdrawal (removal) of groundwater over a period of time that exceeds the recharge rate of the supply aquifer. Also referred to as overdraft or mining the aquifer.

Oxbow: A bow-shaped lake formed in an abandoned meander of a river.

Oxidation: A chemical reaction in which substances combine with oxygen. For example, the combination of iron with oxygen to form an iron oxide.

P

Packer test: An aquifer test performed in an open borehole; the segment of the borehole to be tested is sealed off from the rest of the borehole by inflating seals, called packers, both above and **below** the segment.

Pahoehoe: A Hawaiian term for a lava flow that has a surface flow structure appearance that looks like coiled rope or cord. See aa for contrast.

Paleoclimate: The climate of a given area at a specific time in the past. Paleoclimates can be read from the rocks much as areas with different types of climates produce sediments with specific characteristics today.

Paleocurrent map: A map that shows the directions of currents at the time of sediment deposition. These directions can be determined through the study of cross bedding, ripple marks, tool marks and other sedimentary structures.

Paleohydrology: Study of hydrologic processes and events, using geological, botanical, and cultural evidence, that occurred before the beginning of the systematic collection of hydrologic data and observations.

Paleomagnetism: The study of Earth's magnetic field over time. When rocks that contain magnetic minerals are deposited, the character (vertical and horizontal orientation) of Earth's magnetic field is locked within the rocks. This information can be used to study changes in Earth's magnetic field as well as the movement of plates over time.

Paleontology: The study of ancient life through fossils.

Palaeovalley/paleochannel: Alluvial deposits formed by ancient rivers that are no longer active. These deposits can be buried by other sediments.

Pangaea: A large continental landmass that existed from about 300 million years ago through about 200 million years ago. It included most of the continental lithosphere present at that time. It has since broken up and the fragments have drifted to become the configuration of Earth's present day continents.

Panthalassa: The ancient ocean that surrounded the Pangaea landmass.

Parallel flow paths: Layers of groundwater flow that do not mix with other flow layers because groundwater movement is too slow to create sufficient turbulence to cause mixing to occur. This becomes an important factor in the location and movement of contaminants that enter the groundwater.

Parametric: A parametric drawing is linked to the model. As the model changes, the drawing updates automatically to reflect the change.

Parsimony: The parsimony principle implies that a conceptual model has been simplified as much as possible, yet it retains enough complexity so that it adequately represents the physical system and its behaviour.

Particle count: The results of microscopic examination of treated water with a 'particle counter' – an instrument that classifies suspended particles by number and size.

Palustrine wetlands: Freshwater wetlands including open water bodies of less than 8 hectares in which water is less than 2 metres deep; includes marshes, wet meadows, fens, playas, potholes, pocosins, bogs, swamps, and shallow ponds; most wetlands are in the Palustrine system.

Part per million (ppm): Unit of concentration equal to one milligram per kilogram or one milligram per litre.

Particulate: Fine sands, decayed vegetable matter and other such detritus commonly found in water.

Partition coefficient (Kow): This coefficient provides direct measurement of hydrophobicity of partitioning tendency of chemical between water and an organic phase.

Pathogen: A disease-producing organism that can cause sickness and sometimes death through the consumption of water, including bacteria (such as *Escherichia coli*), protozoa (such as *Cryptosporidium* and *Giardia*) and viruses.

Peak flow: The maximum instantaneous discharge of a stream at a specific location. Corresponds to the highest stage of a flood.

Peak stage: Maximum height of a water surface above an established datum plane. Same as peak gauge height.

Peat: A highly organic soil composed of partially decomposed vegetable matter.

Pediment: A broad, gently sloping erosional surface of low local relief adjacent to an eroding cliff or mountain range. The area is likely covered with sediments.

Pegmatite: A very coarse grained igneous rock, normally of granitic composition. Typically forms during the final states of magma chamber crystallization when the high water content solutions allow rapid crystal growth.

Pelagic sediment: A ocean sediment that accumulates far enough from land that detrital materials are a minor component. These sediments are largely composed of the tiny shell debris of radiolarians and foraminifera.

Perched aquifer: A region in the unsaturated zone where the soil or rock may be locally saturated because it overlies a low-permeability unit.

Perched watertable: The surface in a perched aquifer at which the pore pressure is atmospheric.

Percolation - The movement of water, under hydrostatic pressure, through interstices of a rock or soil (except the movement through large openings such as caves).

Perennial stream: - A stream that has water in its channel at all times.

Perforations: A series of openings in a bore casing.

Peridotite: A dark-coloured, coarse-grained igneous rock that is made up mainly of olivine and pyroxene, with very little quartz or feldspar

Permanent wilting point: The soil matric potential below whish plants wilt and foil to recover, even when placed in a humid chamber. This soil matric potential is usually estimated to be 1.5MPa.

Permeable strata: Layers of rock through which water can pass.

Permeability: The measure of the ability of a rock, soil or sediment to transmit a fluid. The magnitude of the permeability depends largely on the porosity of the connectedness of pore spaces.

Permeability, coefficient of (K): See hydraulic conductivity. The coefficient of permeability is the term previously used for hydraulic conductivity. Its use was mostly discarded in the mid 1900's in favour of hydraulic conductivity because of the confusion with intrinsic permeability.

Permeability, intrinsic (k): Intrinsic permeability is a property of the soil/rock matrix. It is a measure of the relative ease with which a medium can transmit a liquid under a specified gradient. It is related only to the matrix grain size and is independent of the fluid passing through it.

Permeate: Treated water after the reverse osmosis process.

Permafrost: Any frozen soil, subsoil, surficial deposit, or bedrock in arctic or subarctic regions where below-freezing temperatures have existed continuously for many thousands of years.

Permeability: The capacity of a rock for transmitting a gas or fluid; a measure of the relative ease with which a porous medium can transmit a liquid or gas.

Permeable: Capable of transmitting a fluid (porous rock, sediment, or soil); the rate at which a fluid moves through rocks or soil.

Permeable layer: A layer of porous material (rock, soil, unconsolidated sediment); in an aquifer, the layer through which water freely passes as it moves through the ground.

PEST: Parameter estimation software for automated groundwater model calibration.

Pesticide: Collective name for a variety of insecticides, fungicides, herbicides, algicides, fumigants and rodenticides used to kill organisms.

Petrochemicals: Organic and inorganic compounds and mixtures that are derived from petroleum. These include: organic chemicals, cyclic inter¬mediates, plastics, resins, synthetic fibers, elastomers, organic dyes, organic pigments, detergents, surface active agents, carbon black, and ammonia.

Petroleum: A group of liquid hydrocarbons that includes: crude oil, lease condensate, unfinished oils, refined products obtained from the processing of crude oil, and natural gas liquids.

Petroleum Assessment Lease (PAL): Once exploration is complete and sufficient resources have been found in an area, a company may apply for an assessment lease. Assessment Lease activities include development of markets and capital for the resources or product, initial design of production and evaluation of production areas.

Petroleum Exploration Licence (PEL): A company is given the legal right to explore a defined area for petroleum. This title is granted first and allows the company exclusive right to the area to conduct activities such as soil samples, desktop studies a din later stages taking samples and ultimately drilling.

Petroleum Production Lease (PPL): Allows a company exclusive rights to extract the resource in the granted area. A PPL will only be granted once a company has demonstrated that the resource is to the benefit to the State and can be extracted safely without endangering people, environmental or heritage areas and infrastructure.

pH: A logarithmic scale for expressing the acidity or alkalinity of a solution. A pH below seven indicates an acidic solution and above seven indicates an alkaline solution.

Phenols: A class of organic compounds containing phenol (C6HSOH) and its derivatives. Used to make resins weed killers, and as a solvent, disinfectant, and chemical intermediate. Some phenols occur naturally in the environment.

Phosphorus: A nutrient essential for growth that can play a key role in stimulating aquatic growth in lakes and streams. Also found in recycled waters, originating principally from detergents, but also from other domestic wastes. A useful plant nutrient that can also cause off-site problems of eutrophication in water bodies.

Photosynthesis: The synthesis of compounds with the aid of light.

Phreatomagmatic: An explosive volcanic eruption initiated by the interaction of magma and water (usually either meteoric or groundwater).

Phreatophytic: Deep-rooted plants (typically trees) that use groundwater.

Phreatophytes: Plants which have their root system extending into the water table.

Phyllite: A foliate metamorphic rock that is made up mainly of very fine-grained mica. The surface of phyllite is typically lustrous and sometimes wrinkled. It is intermediate in grade between slate and schist.

Physical weathering: A general term applied to a variety of weathering processes that result in the particle size reduction of rock materials with no change in composition. Frost action, salt crystal growth and pressure relief fracturing are examples. Also known as mechanical weathering.

Physiographic province: A region in which the land forms are distinctive and differ significantly from those of adjacent regions.

Physiography: A description of the surface features of the Earth, with an emphasis on the origin of landforms.

Phytoplankton: Microscopic (up to 1-2 mm in diameter) free-floating or weakly mobile aquatic plants (e.g. diatoms, dinoflagellates, chlorophytes, blue-greens).

Picocurie (pCi): One trillionth (10^{-12}) of the amount of radioactivity represented by a curie (Ci). A curie is the amount of radioactivity that yields 3.7×10^{10} radioactive disintegrations per second (dps). A picocurie yields 2.22 disintegrations per minute (dpm) or 0.037 dps.

Piezometer: A small diameter bore or tube constructed for the measurement of hydraulic head at a specific depth in an aquifer. In a piezometer, the section of the borehole (the screened section) in contact with the aquifer is usually very short.

Pilot plant: A mini desalination plant which mimics the performance of a full scale facility in evaluation and testing trial.

Pilot Well: A well for gas and water extraction, generally in close proximity to another for the assessment of field potential.

Pioneer plant: Herbaceous annual and perennial seedling plants that colonize bare areas as a first stage in secondary succession.

Pipe: A closed conveyance or carrier regardless of material, size or shape which conveys water typically for supply service. It is also a buried perforated carrier to collect subsurface drainage water.

Piping: Erosion caused by percolating water in a layer of subsoil resulting in caving and in the formation of narrow conduits tunnels, or `pipes', through which soluble or granular soil material is removed.

PJ: Petajoule (1000 Terajoules)

PL: Petroleum Lease. A PL is required to be granted to perit the commercial exploitation of a reserve.

PLA: Petroleum Lease Application

Placer Deposit: A mass of stream sediment that contains an economically significant concentration of mineral particles. This accumulation of mineral particles is a result of their being of high specific gravity or resistant to abrasion. Gold, magnetite, and diamonds can be found in placer deposits.

Plankton: Floating or weakly swimming organisms at the mercy of the waves and currents. Animals of the group are called zooplankton and the plants are called phytoplankton.

Plateau Basalt: A sequence of parallel to subparallel basalt flows that were formed during a geologically brief interval of time and which covered an extensive geographic area. Thought to have formed from simultaneous or successive fissure eruptions.

Playa: Flat-floored centre of undrained desert basin.

Plinian eruption: An explosive eruption where large volumes of rock, ash and gas are blasted at high velocity from a vent. These eruptions produce huge clouds that can rise tens of kilometers into the atmosphere.

Plugged and abandoned: When all the reservoir and high pressure zones in a well are sealed with cement to ensure no fluids can escape.

Plumbness: The horizontal deviation (drift) of the bore centre line from true vertical.

Plume: In groundwater a plume is a of contaminant concentrations created by the movement of groundwater beneath a contaminant source. Contaminants spread mostly laterally in the direction of groundwater movement. The source site has the highest concentration, and the concentration decreases away from the source.

Pluviometer: An instrument that measures both the magnitude and intensity of rainfall.

PN (pipe nominal): The nominal pressure rating of the pipe.

Point-of-use treatment device: A treatment device applied to a single tap used for the purpose of reducing contaminants in drinking water at that one tap.

Point-source contaminant: Any substance that degrades water quality and originates from discrete locations such as discharge pipes, drainage ditches, wells, concentrated livestock operations, or floating craft.

Point source pollution: Pollution originating from a specific localised source, e.g. sewage or effluent discharge, industrial waste discharge.

Polarity Epoch: An interval of time between reversals of Earth's magnetic field.

Polarity Event: A specific event in the history of Earth's magnetic field. Usually used in reference to a specific polarity reversal.

Polarity Reversal: A change in the polarity of Earth's magnetic field in which the north magnetic pole becomes the south magnetic pole and vice versa. Also known as geomagnetic reversal or magnetic reversal. Earth's magnetic field has reversed many times in the past and the time intervals between these changes are known as polarity epochs.

Pollutant: Substance that damages the quality of the environment.

Pollute: To make foul or unclean; dirty.

Pollution: Water pollution occurs when waste products or other substances (effluent, litter, refuse, sewage or contaminated runoff) change the physical, chemical or biological properties of the water, adversely affecting water quality, living species and beneficial uses.

Pollutant: Any substance that, when present in a hydrologic system at sufficient concentration, degrades water quality in ways that are or could become harmful to human and/or ecological health or that impair the use of water for recreation, agriculture, industry, commerce, or domestic purposes.

Polychlorinated biphenyls (PCBs): A mixture of chlorinated derivatives of biphenyl, marketed under the trade name Aroclor with a number designating the chlorine content (such as Aroclor 1260). PCBs were used in transformers and capacitors for insulating purposes and in gas pipeline systems as a lubricant. Further sale for new use was banned by law in 1979.

Polycyclic aromatic hydrocarbon (PAH): A class of organic compounds with a fused-ring aromatic structure. PAHs result from incomplete combustion of organic carbon (including wood), municipal solid waste, and fossil fuels, as well as from natural or anthropogenic introduction of uncombusted coal and oil. PAHs include benzo(a)pyrene, fluoranthene, and pyrene.

Polymerase chain reaction (PCR): A method for detecting organisms/biological particles by detecting and amplifying DNA sequences.

Pondage test: A water balance approach to measuring channel seepage within an isolated reach of channel. A section of channel is blocked off with embankments and the section filled with water. The seepage rate is calculated from the rate of water drop after corrections are made for evaporation and rainfall.

Ponding: Water gathering in a depression (e.g. on a roof) from which it cannot drain away.

Pool: A small part of a stream reach with little velocity, commonly with water deeper than surrounding areas.

Population: A collection of individuals of one species or mixed species making up the residents of a prescribed area.

Porosity: The ratio of the volume of voids in a rock or soil to the total volume. Porosity is dimensionless and is normally expressed as a percentage.

Porosity, Effective: The volume of the inter-connected void spaces through which water or other fluids can travel in a rock or sediment divided by the total volume of the rock or sediment.

Porosity, Primary: The porosity that represents the original pore openings when a rock or sediment formed.

Porosity, Secondary: The porosity that has been caused by fractures or weathering in a rock or sediment after it has been formed.

Pore space: The pores in a rock or soil considered collectively. Also known as pore volume, void space or interstices.

Pore water pressure: The hydrostatic pressure of water stored in the pores and interstices of a porous medium.

Porous media: Media which contain spaces between grains of sand and gravel. They include unconsolidated sands and gravels and consolidated sandstones.

Post-audit: Comparison of model predictions with what actually happened. (For further information refer also to section 7.4 of the MDBA Model guidelines, especially the cautionary comments)

Postemergence herbicide: Herbicide applied to foliage after the crop has sprouted to kill or significantly retard the growth of weeds.

Potable (drinking) water: Water of a quality suitable for drinking.

Potential evapotranspiration: The amount of moisture which, if available, would be removed from a given land area by evapotranspiration; expressed in units of water depth.

Potentiometric level: The potential level to which water will rise in a bore/well that penetrates an aquifer; if the potentiometric level is higher than the land surface, a bore/well drilled at that site will overflow. See artesian well and confined aquifer. The water table is the potentiometric surface for an unconfined aquifer.

Potentiometric surface: An imaginary surface that represents the total head at all points in an aquifer. It represents the height above a datum plane at which the water level stands in tightly cased bores/wells that penetrate the aquifer.

Pothole: A cylindrical or hemispherical hold in the bedrock of a stream that is formed from the continual swirling motion of sand and gravel by swirling currents.

Precipitation: (1) Any or all forms of water particles that fall from the atmosphere, such as rain, snow, hail, and sleet. (2) The act or process of producing a solid phase within a liquid medium.

Pre-emergence herbicide: Herbicide applied to bare ground after planting the crop but prior to the crop sprouting above ground to kill or significantly retard the growth of weed seedlings.

Pre-filtration: A process to remove particulate from 'raw' water prior to the reverse osmosis treatment stage. This can involve passage through media such as sand, gravel or can be membrane based.

Preventive measure: Any planned action, activity or process that is used to prevent hazards from occurring or reduce them to acceptable levels.

Primary Recovery: Any crude oil or natural gas that is recovered from a well as a result of the natural pressure within the reservoir.

Primary sedimentation: Initial treatment of wastewater involving screening and sedimentation to remove solids.

Primary Seismic Waves: The fastest set of earthquake vibrations - also known as P-waves. They move through the Earth in compression and expansion motions (much like sound waves move through air). Called primary because they are the first recorded at a seismograph. Primary waves are able to travel through both solids and liquids.

Primary treatment: The first major treatment process in a sewage treatment facility, principally designed to remove a substantial amount of suspended matter, but little or no colloidal or dissolved matter. Typical primary sewage treatment processes may include clarification (with or without chemical treatment, to accomplish solid-liquid separation), grease removal and screens.

Pristine: The earliest condition of the quality of a water body; unaffected by human activities.

Probability Distribution Function (pdf): A graph or formula which expresses the probability that an uncertain parameter will have a particular value.

Process design: Activities involved in determining the technical, engineering and implementation requirements for specific water treatment applications and processes.

Process water: Water used in industrial or manufacturing processes.

Produced water: Pumping groundwater from a coal seam reduces the pressure that keeps the natural gas in place. Reducing the pressure allows the gas and 'produced' groundwater to flow into the well and up to the surface. The water contained in coal seams may be brackish, salty or even fresh. If necessary, the water is treated and recycled for use in industry or irrigation.

Production zone: The zone within the target formation that produces the water supply requirements for the bore.

Prograding: Seward build-up of beach, delta or fan by near shore deposition of sediments.

Prospecting: The activities associated with the search for an area of probable mineralization. It can include: topographical, geological, geochemical and geophysical studies. Prospecting is usually done prior to the acquisition of mineral rights.

Proto-sun: An intermediate stage in the development of a star in which a large cloud of dust and gases gradually condenses through gravitational actions.

Protozoa: A phylum of single-celled organisms.

Proven, probable and possible reserves: Proven and probable reserves plus reserves that are deemed possible (at least 10% likely) to be commercially recoverable. Also knows as 3P or P10 reserves.

Proven and probable reserves: Proven reserves plus reserves that are deemed probably (at least 50% likely) to be commercially recoverable. Also known as 2P or P50 reserves.

Proven reserves: Mineral deposits that have been explored thoroughly enough to be quantified (at least 90% likely) but which are still in the ground. Also known as 1P or P90 reserves.

PRRT: Petroleum Resource Rent Tax

psi: Pound per square inch. Also known as – lbf/in2. It s a traditional unit of pressure

Pumice: A vesicular volcanic glass of granitic composition. It has so many vesicles that it has a very low specific gravity - sometimes low enough to float on water.

Public drinking water source area (PDWSA): Includes all underground water pollution control areas, catchment areas and water reserves constituted under the *Metropolitan Water Supply Sewerage and Drainage Act* 1909 (WA) and *the Country Areas Water Supply Act 1947* (WA).

The Department of Water's policy for the protection of PDWSAs includes a system that defines three specific priority areas:

Priority 1 (P1): They have the fundamental water quality objective or risk avoidance (e.g. state forest and other crown land).

Priority 2 (P2): They have the fundamental water quality objective or risk minimisation (e.g. land that is zoned rural).

Priority 3 (P3): They have the fundamental water quality objective of risk management (e.g. areas zoned urban or light/general industrial).

Public sector circular number 88: A state government circular produced by the Department of Health providing guidance on appropriate herbicide use within water catchment areas.

Public-supply withdrawals: Water withdrawn by public and private water suppliers for use within a general community. Water is used for a variety of purposes such as domestic, commercial, industrial, and public water use.

Pumping level: The water level in the bore when pumping is in progress.

Pumping test: Also known as an aquifer test. A test made by pumping a well for a period of time at a measured rate and observing the change in hydraulic head in the aquifer. A pumping test may be used to determine the capacity of the well and the hydraulic characteristics of the aquifer.

Punch Hole: A small diameter hole which is drilled to confirm the exact depth of an underground structure or seam.

PVC-U: Unplasticised polyvinyl chloride.

P-wave: Primary seismic waves. The fastest set of earthquake vibrations. They move through the Earth in compression and expansion motions (much like sound waves move through air). Called primary because they are the first recorded at a seismograph. Primary waves are able to travel through both solids and liquids.

Pyroclastic Flow: A hot, high-velocity mixture of ash, gas and fragmented rock that flows like a liquid down slopes and over terrain.

Pyroclastic Rock: A rock formed when small particles of magma are blown from the vent of a volcano by escaping gas.

Pyroxene Granulite: A coarse-grained contact metamorphic rock that is formed at high temperatures and low pressures and which is rich in pyroxene minerals.

Q

Qanat: A qanat is a very old (thousands of years) water management system used to provide a reliable supply of water to human settlements and for irrigation in hot, arid and semi-arid climates such as Iran, Syria and Jordan. It consists of an infiltration gallery which intersects the groundwater and enables the water to flow under gravity to the point of abstraction.

Quality: The totality of characteristics of an entity that bear on its ability to satisfy stated and implied needs; the term 'quality' should not be used to express a degree of excellence.

Quality assurance (QA): Evaluation of quality-control data to allow quantitative determination of the quality of chemical data collected during a study. Techniques used to collect, process, and analyse water samples are evaluated.

Quality control (QC): Operational techniques and activities that are used to fulfil requirements for quality.

Quality management: Includes both quality control and quality assurance, as well as additional concepts of quality policy, quality planning and quality improvement. Quality management operates throughout the quality system.

Quality system: Organisational structure, procedures, processes and resources needed to implement quality management.

Quarry: A surface mine usually for the extraction of construction stone.

Quartz: One of the most abundant minerals in the earth's crust. Has a chemical composition of SiO2 and a hardness of seven. One of the index minerals in Moh's Hardness Scale. Occurs in sedimentary, metamorphic and igneous rocks.

Quartz Arenite: A sandstone consisting of at least 95% quartz.

Quartzite: A metamorphic rock formed by the alteration of sandstone by heat, pressure and chemical activity.

Quartzose: An adjective used in reference to a rock that is composted primarily of quartz.

Quicksand: A bed of sand that has a high water content. The water within the sand is often flowing through the spaces between the sand grains. This creates a soft, fluid-like material that yields easily to pressure and in which heavy objects will sink.

Quicksilver: A nickname for the element mercury.

R

Radial drainage: A drainage pattern in which stream channels run away from a central high point such as a volcano or dome.

Radiolarian: A group of one-celled marine animals with a siliceous skeleton that occupies shallow portions of the water column. Radiolarians have a range from Cambrian to present.

Radiolarian ooze: A deep-sea pelagic sediment that contains at least 30% siliceous radiolarian remains.

Radionuclide: An isotope of an element that is unstable and undergoes radioactive decay.

Radon: A naturally occurring, colourless, odourless, radioactive gas formed by the disintegration of the element radium; It is damaging to human lungs when inhaled.

Radial collector well: A large diameter well with horizontal bores extending outwards into the aquifer. Also known as a Ranney well.

Rain: Water drops falling from the sky to the earth, being condensed from the aqueous vapour in the atmosphere.

Rain shadow: A dry region on the lee side of a topographic obstacle, usually a mountain range, where rainfall is noticeably less than on the windward side.

Rainfall on storage: The average depth of rainfall over a period of time on the storage water surface.

Rainfall intensity: Rainfall depth per unit time

Rainfall Residual Mass Curve (RRMC): A plot against time of the cumulative deviation of the actual monthly rainfall from the mean rainfall for each month over the period of record. Positive slopes of the RRMC indicate periods of above average rainfall and negative slopes indicate periods of below average rainfall.

Raster data: A gridded dataset which stores values at each grid cell. Digital images and DEMs are examples of raster data.

Rational method: A simple method of computing peak runoff for small watersheds. The method takes into account watershed area, rainfall intensity, and a runoff coefficient, which is used to estimate losses.

Raw water: Water prior to reverse osmosis treatment, also known as feed water or intake water.

Reach: A continuous part of a stream between two specified points.

Re-aeration: The replenishment of oxygen in water from which oxygen has been removed.

Readily available water: Water that can be removed from a soil horizon by a crop without resulting water deficit stress. This is often estimated to half the "total available water".

Recessional moraine: An end moraine built during a temporary but significant pause in the final retreat of a glacier.

Recharge (groundwater): Is the action of water infiltrating through the soil/ground to replenish an aquifer.

Recharge area: The geographic area where water infiltrates into the ground and enters an aquifer.

Recharge boundary: An aquifer system boundary that adds water to the aquifer. Streams and lakes are typically recharge boundaries.

Recharge rate: The quantity of water per unit of time that replenishes an aquifer.

Recharge zone or area: An area through which water from a groundwater catchment percolates to replenish (recharge) an aquifer. An unconfined aquifer is recharged by rainfall throughout its distribution. Confined aquifers are recharged in specific areas where water leaks from overlaying aquifers, or where the aquifer rises to meet the surface.

Reclaimed wastewater: Treated wastewater that can be used for beneficial purposes, such as irrigating certain plants; alternative but less accurate term for treated wastewater.

Reconditioning: Restoring a bore by a variety of chemical or mechanical means that do not involve replacing or modifying any of the original materials used to construct the bore.

Recovery: The distance that the water level rises above its pumping level at a given time after pumping ceased. It is the difference between the Residual Drawdown after the given time and the hypothetical drawdown if pumping had not ceased. When the water level returns to S.W.L. recovery is said to be complete.

Recrystallisation: A solid state reaction in which the atoms of existing crystals within a rock are reorganized in response to heat and/or pressure. The recrystallised mineral grains are typically larger in size than the original crystals.

Rectangular Drainage: A drainage pattern in which stream channels develop within a large-scale network of intersecting joints. This drainage pattern is characterized by right-angle bends in the channels of streams and streams that intersect at right angles.

Recurrence interval: The average interval of time within which the magnitude of a given event, such as a storm or flood, will be equalled or exceeded once.

Recycled water: Water that is used more than one time before it passes back into the natural hydrologic system. Can also be called re-use water and refers to wastewater that has been collected and treated to a quality standard that enables it to be used for a specific purpose. Examples include cooling water for power generation, irrigation and beneficial release to the environment.

Reduced water level: Groundwater levels give with respect to height above sea-level (i.e. given mAHD).

Refractory: A stable material difficult to convert or remove entirely from wastewater.

Regional groundwater systems: Extensive aquifers which take longer than local systems to respond to increased groundwater recharge because their recharge and discharge sites are separated by large distances (>10 km), and/or they have a deep water table. Unconfined aquifers with deep water tables that are part of regional flow systems may become, in effect, local flow systems if there is sufficient recharge to cause the water table to rise close to the surface (<5m).

Regolith: The layer or mantle of fragmented and unconsolidated rock material, residual or transported, that nearly everywhere forms the surface of the land and overlies or covers the bedrock.

Regression: A retreat of the sea from land areas. Possible causes include a drop in sea level or uplift.

Regulated river network: A water supply network which at its simplest may comprise a single structure, such as a dam, which provides storage and the ability to regulate or control river flows, but which may compromise many structures and multiple connected regulated rivers or streams. A regulated river network would typically provide a regulated river supply service to a variety of rural, commercial or urban supply customers.

Regulated system: River system where the flow of the water is regulated through the operation of large dams or weirs.

Regulation (of a stream): Artificial manipulation of the flow of a stream.

Regulator: A state or territory water licensing authority.

Rehabilitation: The restoration of a bore to its most efficient condition using a variety of chemical or mechanical techniques, which may include replacing the production casing and/or screens. A driller shall be licensed in order to carry out rehabilitation of a bore.

Reject water: Water containing salts or particulate from the treatment process that has not beneficial use. Can also be referred to as RO concentrate.

Relative abundance: The number of organisms of a particular kind present in a sample relative to the total number of organisms in the sample.

Relative density or specific gravity: The ratio of the density of a substance to the density of water.

Relief: Variations in the height and slope of Earth's surface. Also used in reference to the vertical difference between the highest and lowest elevations of an area.

Remediation: Containment, treatment or removal of contaminated groundwater. May also include containment, treatment or removal of contaminated soil above the water table.

Remote Sensing Techniques: Remote sensing is the small- or large-scale acquisition of information of an object or phenomenon, by the use of either recording or real-time sensing device(s) that are wireless, or not in physical or intimate contact with the object (such as by way of aircraft, spacecraft, satellite, buoy, or ship). Digital information representing characteristics of the Earth's surface or sub-surface properties can be acquired in this manner.

Renewable groundwater: Groundwater extracted from an aquifer that receives recharge from rivers, rainfall, or from other aquifers.

Replacement: The dissolving or disintegration of one material followed by precipitation of a new material in its place.

Representative sample: A portion of material or water that is as nearly identical in content and consistency as possible to that in the larger body of material or water being sampled.

Reserve: A resources which has been quantified by a verifiable process and has demonstrated commercial value.

Reservoir: A rock or geological formation that holds a fluid within the pore spaces between the individual grains; any natural or artificial holding area used to store, regulate or control water.

Residence time: Period of time that groundwater remains in an aquifer.

Residential water use: See Domestic withdrawals.

Residual: The difference between the computed and observed value of a variable at a specific time and location.

Residual Drawdown: The distance that the water level in a bore/well remains lowered from the S.W.L. after pumping ceases. It is measured at specified times after pumping stopped.

Residual risk: The risk remaining after consideration of existing preventive measures.

Resistivity survey: A geophysical technique used to measure the apparent resistivity of the subsurface by applying a direct current to the ground and measuring the resultant ground potential and current in the vicinity of the applied current.

Resource: An unquantified body of material of potential value.

RET: Renewable Energy Target

Retrograde metamorphism: Mineral changes within a rock that are caused by adjustments to conditions of reduced temperature and pressure.

Return flow: (1) That part of a diverted flow that is not consumptively used and returned to its original source or another body of water. (2) Irrigation water that is applied to an area and which is not consumed in evaporation or transpiration and returns to a surface stream or aquifer.

Reuse water: Re-using water that would otherwise be wasted instead of using fresh water. Reuse water includes wastewater, stormwater, rainwater and grey-water.

Reverse osmosis (RO): A liquid filtration method with removes many types of large atomic molecules from smaller molecules, by forcing the liquid at high pressure through a membrane with pores (holes) just big enough to allow the small molecules to pass through.

Rhyolite: The fine-grained volcanic or extrusive rocks that are equivalent in composition to granite. Normally white, pink or gray in colour.

Richter magnitude scale: A scale that is used to compare the strength of earthquakes based upon the amount of energy released. The scale is logarithmic and an arbitrary earthquake was used as a starting point for creating the scale. As a result it is a continuous scale with no upper limit and negative numbers possible for very small earthquakes. An upper limit of approximately 9.0 is suspected as Earth materials will most likely fail before storing enough energy for a larger magnitude earthquake.

Ridge (mid-ocean): An elevated area of the sea floor in the center of an ocean basin with rugged topography, a central rift-valley and recurring seismic activity. Ridges generally stand about 1000 meters to 3000 meters above the adjacent ocean floor and are about 1500 kilometers in width.

Right-lateral fault: A fault with horizontal movement. If you are standing on one side of the fault and look across it, the block on the opposite side of the fault has moved to the right.

Rip current: A strong, narrow current of high velocity and short duration that flows seaward through the breaker zone. Caused when a build up of water pushed onto the beach by winds and waves returns seaward.

Ripple marks: A series of parallel or sub-parallel ridges in sand or sediment that is caused by the rhythmic or directional movement of wind or water.

Riparian: Pertaining to or situated on the bank of a natural body of flowing water.

Riparian rights: A concept of water law under which authorization to use water in a stream is based on ownership of the land adjacent to the stream.

Riparian zone: Pertaining to or located on the bank of a body of water, especially a stream.

Risk: The likelihood of a hazard causing harm in exposed populations in a specified time frame, including the magnitude of that harm.

Risk assessment: The likelihood of a hazard causing harm in exposed populations in a specified time frame, including the magnitude of that harm.

Risk management: The systematic evaluation of the water supply system, the identification of hazards and hazardous events, the assessment of risks and the development and implementation of preventive strategies to manage the risks.

River: A considerable nature stream of water flowing in a definite course or channel or series of diverging and converging channels.

Riverine wetlands: Wetlands within river and stream channels; ocean-derived salinity is less than 500 part per million.

River channel storage: Volume of water in river channels. Includes the instantaneous volume of moving water, and any water in weirs which are not classed as major on-river storages or minor on-stream dams.

RMA2: A 2D hydrodynamic depth averaged flow model developed by the U.S. Army Corps of Engineers. Included as part of the TABS-MD modelling suite and as part of SMS.

RMA4: A 2D hydrodynamic depth averaged constituent transport model developed by the U.S. Army Corps of Engineers. Included as part of the TABS-MD modelling suite and as part of SMS.

RO: Reverse Osmosis

Rock: Any naturally formed, consolidated or unconsolidated material (but not soil) consisting of two or more minerals.

Rock cycle: All rock at or near Earth's surface is being modified by the processes of metamorphism, melting, crystallization, lithification and weathering. These processes move rock material through the states of metamorphic rock, igneous rock, sedimentary rock, melts and sediment. The natural and continuous cycling of rock materials through these states is known as the rock cycle.

Rock Flour: Finely pulverized rock material of silt or smaller size produced by abrasion at the base of a glacier.

Rock Glacier: A mass of rock material, cemented together by ice, that flows down a slope under the force of gravity much like the motion of a glacier

Rock, Igneous: A rock formed by the cooling and crystallisation of a molten rock mass called magma.

Rock, Metamorphic: A rock formed by the application of heat and pressure to preexisting rocks.

Rock Salt: A chemical sedimentary rock that forms from the evaporation of ocean or saline lake waters. It is also known by the mineral name "halite". It is rarely found at Earth's surface, except in areas of very arid climate. It is often mined for use in the chemical industry or for use as a winter highway treatment. Some halite is processed for use as a seasoning for food

Rock, Sedimentary: A layered rock formed from the consolidation of sediment. Includes clastic rocks (such as sandstone), rocks formed by chemical precipitation in water (such as limestone), or rocks formed from organic material (such as coal).

Rock, Volcanic: An igneous rock formed when molten rock called lava cools on the earth's surface.

Rockslide: A type of mass wasting in which a large volume of rock debris slides down a slope under the influence of gravity.

Routing: See flow routing.

RT3D: Quasi 3D groundwater reactive transport model used with MODLFOW.

Runoff: Water that flows over the surface from a catchment area, including streams.

Rupture strength: The maximum amount of stress that a material can sustain without failure.

Rural withdrawals: Water used in suburban or farm areas for domestic and livestock needs. The water generally is self- supplied and includes domestic use, drinking water for livestock, and other uses such as dairy sanitation, evaporation from stock-watering ponds, and cleaning and waste disposal.

Water Resources: Glossary of Terms

S

Safe yield: See sustainable yield.

Salina clusters: Group of salt lakes, typically groundwater discharge lakes.

Saline water: Water that is considered unsuitable for human consumption or for irrigation because of its high content of dissolved solids; generally expressed as milligrams per litre (mg/L) of dissolved solids; seawater is generally considered to contain more than 35,000 mg/L of dissolved solids. A general salinity scale is:

	Concentration of dissolved solids in milligrams per litre
Slightly Saline	1,000 - 3,000
Moderately Saline	3,000 - 10,000
Very Saline	10,000 - 35,000
Brine	More than 35,000

Salinity: The concentration of sodium chloride or dissolved salts in water, usually expressed in EC units or milligrams of total dissolved solids per litre (mg/L TDS). The conversion factor of 0.6 mg/L TDS = 1 EC unit is commonly used as an approximation.

Salinization: The condition in which the salt content of soil accumulates over time to above normal levels; occurs in some parts of the world where water containing high salt concentration evaporates from fields irrigated with standing water.

Salt marsh: A low coastal grassland frequently inundated by the tide.

Salt water: Water that contains a relatively high percentage (over 500 parts per million) of salt minerals.

Salt water intrusion: Saltwater intrusion is the movement of saline water into freshwater aquifers. It can result as a consequence of construction of navigation channels or oil field canals. Saltwater intrusion occurs in virtually all coastal aquifers, where they are in hydraulic continuity with seawater. The density differential between seawater and fresh water results in a wedge of seawater forming naturally in the aquifer. Over pumping of groundwater from coastal bores/wells causes the wedge to move inland; recharge of the fresh water makes it move towards the sea.

Saltation: The transport of sediment in short jumps and bounces above the stream bed or ground by a current that is not strong enough to hold the sediment in continuous suspension. (See suspension and traction for comparison.)

Sandstone: A sedimentary rock composed of sand-sized particles (1/16 to 2 millimetres in diameter).

Sandy soils: Soils with a clay content below 16%.

Sanitary survey: A review of the water sources, facilities, equipment, operation and maintenance of a public water system to evaluate its adequacy for producing and distributing safe drinking water.

Saturated thickness: Total water-bearing thickness of an aquifer.

Saturated zone: A subsurface zone in which all the interstices or voids are filled with water under pressure greater than that of the atmosphere. See also Water table.

Scheme supply: Water diverted from a source or sources by a water authority or private company and supplied via a distribution network to customers for urban and industrial use or for irrigation.

Schist: A metamorphic rock containing abundant particles of mica, characterized by strong foliation, and originating from a metamorphism in which directed pressure plays a significant role.

Schistosity: The parallel arrangement of platy or prismatic minerals in a rock that is caused by metamorphism in which directed pressure plays a significant role.

Scoria: An igneous rock of basaltic composition and containing numerous vesicles caused by trapped gases.

Screen: A special form of bore liner used to stabilise the aquifer or gravel pack, which allowing the flow of water through the bore into the casing and permitting development of the screened formation by an appropriate process.

Sea level: Normally refers to the long-term average position of the sea surface. Sea level varies from place to place and with the time period for which the average is calculated.

Sea water: Water from the sea. Sea water is generally considered to contain more than 35,000 mg/L of dissolved solids and have a relative density of 1.025 although these values vary from place to place throughout the planet.

Sea-floor spreading: The process that occurs at mid-ocean ridges in which convection currents below pull the plates apart and create new sea floor.

Seamount: A mountain on the sea floor that has at least 1000 meters of local relief. Most seamounts are shield volcanoes.

Secondary effluent: The liquid portion of wastewater leaving secondary treatment.

Secondary treatment: Typically, a biological treatment process that is designed to remove approximately 85% of the Biological Oxygen Demand (BOD) and influent suspended solids. Some nutrients may incidentally be removed, and ammonia may be converted to nitrate. Typical secondary sewage treatment processes may include sand filtration, disinfection, a polishing step (to lower suspended solids and bacterial levels), activated-sludge processes, anaerobic plus aerobic processes, biological filters and lagoons (aerated, facultative, maturation or polishing).

Sediment: Particles, derived from rocks or biological materials that have been transported by a fluid or other natural process, suspended or settled in water.

Sediment transport: The physical process of transport of sediments in hydrodynamic flows. Also can reference numerical models which model these processes.

Sedimentary aquifers: These occur in consolidated sediments such as porous sandstones and conglomerates, in which water is stored in the inter-granular pores, and limestone, in which water is stored in solution cavities and joints. These aquifers are generally located in sedimentary basins that are continuous over large areas *and* may be tens or hundreds of metres thick. In terms of quantity, they contain the largest groundwater resources.

Sedimentary basins: Relatively large areas where thick layers of sedimentary rock such as sandstone, siltstone and conglomerate have been deposited over many years.

Sedimentary rocks: Rocks formed by the consolidation of loose sediment that has accumulated in layers.

Sedimentary structure: A structure in a sedimentary rock that forms at or near the time of deposition and reveals information about the depositional environment. Examples include: ripple marks, cross-bedding, mud cracks, and graded bedding.

Sedimentation: The act or process of forming or accumulating sediment in layers; the process of deposition of sediment.

Seep: A small area where water percolates (see percolation) slowly to the land surface.

Seepage: (1) The slow movement of water into or out of a body of surface or subsurface water. (2) The loss of water by infiltration into the soil from a canal, ditch, lateral, watercourse, reservoir, storage facility, or other body of water, or from a field.

Seepage meter: Covered cylindrical infiltrometers modified for use under water. Seepage meters are used for spot measurements of seepage in channels without artificial lining. The most well know seepage meter is the "Idaho Meter".

Seepage plume: The horizontal and vertical extent of groundwater which has been mixed with channel seepage water.

Seepage velocity: Also known as pore water velocity. The rate of movement of fluid particles through porous media along a line from one point to another.

Seiche: A sudden oscillation of the water in a moderate-size body of water, caused by wind.

Seif dune: A large sand dune that forms parallel to the direction of a strong wind that blows in a consistent direction throughout the year. Also called a longitudinal dune.

Seismic: An assessment process whereby the reflected vibrations from a series of shocks or vibrations on the surface ware used to infer underground structures.

Seismic discontinuity: A surface separating rocks that transmit seismic waves at different velocities.

Seismic survey: A method of determining sub-surface features by sending shock waves into rock layers and measuring the time it takes to return to the surface.

Seismicity: The study of the worldwide distribution of earthquakes over time and the probability of an earthquake occurring in a specific location.

Selective herbicide: A compound that kills or significantly retards unwanted plant species without significantly damaging desired plant species.

Self-extracted water: Water that is extracted by the user (generally in-situ) from either surface waters (streams or dams) or groundwater bores.

Semivolatile organic compound (SVOC): Operationally defined as a group of synthetic organic compounds that are solvent-extractable and can be determined by gas chromatography/mass spectrometry. SVOCs include phenols, phthalates, and Polycyclic aromatic hydrocarbons (PARS).

Semi-Confined aquifer: See leaky aquifer.

Sensitivity analysis: The measurement of the uncertainty in a calibrated model as a function of uncertainty in estimates of aquifer parameters and boundary conditions.

Septic system: Used to treat household sewage and wastewater by allowing the solids to decompose and settle in a tank, then letting the liquid be absorbed by the soil in a drainage field. Septic systems are used when a sewer line is not available to carry wastes to a sewage treatment plan. Also called an onsite wastewater treatment system.

Sequestration: The process of removing carbon from the atmosphere. Generally, sequestration is achieved through establishing tree plantations; however it can also be accomplished by other means, including chemical treatment and deep ocean air injection.\

Service reservoir / tank: A storage for drinking water, generally within the distribution system, used to meet fluctuating demands, accommodate emergency requirements and/or equalise operating pressures.

Settling pond: An open pond where waste or process water is allowed to stand while suspended materials settle out.

Sewage: The waste matter which passes through sewers; Material collected from internal household and other building drains. Includes faecal waster and urine from toilets, shower and bath water, laundry water and kitchen water.

Sewer: An artificial conduit, usually underground, for carrying off waste water and refuse, as from a town or city.

Sewer mining: Process of extracting wastewater directly from a sewer, either before or after a sewage treatment plant, for reuse as recycled water.

Sewer reticulation main: Sewer reticulation mains include all gravity sewer mains, all pressure mains (including common effluent pipelines, rising mains etc) and all vacuum systems mains of any diameter. This excludes property connection sewers and pipelines carrying treated effluent.

Shale: A fine-grained sedimentary rock formed by the consolidation of clay, silt, or mud.

Shale gas: Another form of natural gas occurring in shale formations.

Shallows: A term applied to a shallow place or area in a body of water; a shoal.

Shandying: Addition of one water source to another, which modifies the quality of the water.

Shapefile: A file format used by programs with Geographic Information Systems (GIS) capability that links geometric features with a database of information.

Shoal: A relatively shallow place in a stream, lake, or sea.

Shoe: An extension fitted to the end of the casing, commonly a drive show (for advancing the casing) or a flat shoe (used for grouting).

Shotcrete: A hard surface lining (with or without fibres) formed by the spraying of a concrete that dries in place onto the surface of the channel subgrade to form a hard surface and seal the channel.

Shrubland: Land covered predominantly with shrubs.

Sideslope gradient: The representative change in elevation in a given horizontal distance (usually about 300 yards) perpendicular to a stream; the valley slope along a line perpendicular to the stream (near a water-quality or biological sampling point).

Siliciclastic rocks: Rocks such as shale and sandstone that are formed by the compaction and cementation of quartz-rich mineral grains.

Siltation: The deposition or accumulation of silt (or small-grained material) in a body of water.

Siltstone: A clastic sedimentary rock that forms from silt-size (between 1/256 and 1/16 millimetre diameter) weathering debris.

Silviculture: The cultivation of forest trees.

Simulation: One complete execution of a groundwater modelling program, including input and output.

Simplicity: The simplicity (or parsimony) principle implies that a conceptual model has been simplified as much as possible, yet it retains enough complexity so that it adequately represents the physical system and its behaviour.

Sinkhole: A depression in an area underlain by limestone. Its drainage is subterranean.

Sinuosity: The ratio of the channel length between two points on a channel to the straight-line distance between the same two points; a measure of meandering.

Skewness: Numerical measure of the lack of symmetry of an asymmetrical frequency distribution.

Slate: A foliated metamorphic rock that is formed through the metamorphism of shale. It is a low grade metamorphic rock that splits into thin pieces.

Slough: A small marshy tract lying in a swale or other local shallow, undrained depression; a sluggish creek or channel in a wetland.

Slug test: One of several methods used to evaluate the permeability (or hydraulic conductivity) of an aquifer. The procedure involved either adding or removing a measured quantity of water from a well rapidly, followed by making a rapid series of water-level measurements to assess the rate of water-level recovery (either rising-head or falling-head).

SMS: Surface water Modelling System

Snowpack: Volume of water held as snow.

Sodicity: This is a condition where the positively charged sodium ions cause the soil particles to repel each other, resulting in soil swelling, dispersion and reduced soil permeability.

Sodium: An element found endemic in the environment. High concentrations of sodium in soil relative to calcium and magnesium cause sodicity (ESP >6 or SAR >3).

Soil: The top layer of the Earth's surface that supports plant growth. It contains unconsolidated rock and mineral particles mixed with organic material.

Soil ameliorant: Product that can be added to soils to improve chemical or physical properties (examples include using lime to increase pH, or dolomite or gypsum to reduce soil sodicity).

Soil horizon: A layer of soil that is distinguishable from adjacent layers by characteristic physical and chemical properties.

Soil sealants: Soil sealants are either natural or artificially processed materials that can be either injected into water, mixed into the soil, sprayed onto the soil or injected into the subsoil to reduce the channel seepage losses and increase soil stability.

Soil moisture: Water occurring in the pore spaces between the soil particles in the unsaturated zone from which water is discharged by the transpiration of plants or by evaporation from the soil.

Soil sorption coefficient (K_d): This is the ratio of sorbed to solution pesticide in a water-soil slurry. It is a measure of the relative affinities of the pesticide for water and a soil surface.

Soil sorption coefficient (K_{oc}): This adjusts KD for the proportion of organic carbon in the soil.

Sole source aquifer: An aquifer that supplies 50% or more of the drinking water of an area.

Solvent: See Solution.

Solution: Formed when a solid, gas, or another liquid in contact with a liquid becomes dispersed homogeneously throughout the liquid. The substance, called a solute, is said to dissolve. The liquid is called the solvent.

Sonic drilling: A continuous core drilling method that uses vibrosonic energy to pulverize drilled material and push it outwards from the borehole. This permits the hole to be advanced without requiring a drilling fluid to remove cuttings back to the surface. Commonly used for environmental investigation.

Sorb: To take up and hold either by absorption or adsorption.

Sorption: General term for the interaction (binding or association) of a solute ion or molecule with a solid.

Sorted: A measure of the uniformity of grain sizes.

Source rocks: The rocks from which fragments and other detached pieces have been derived to form a different rock.

Source water: Water extracted from a particular location such as groundwater, aquifers, rivers or the sea, notably before any treatment to make it suitable for drinking.

Source water assessment: A process in which the land area that impacts a public drinking water source is delineated, possible sources of contaminants that could impact that drinking water source are identified, and a determination of the likelihood that the contaminants will reach the drinking water source is made. See source water protection.

Source water protection: Voluntary action taken to prevent the pollution of drinking water sources, including groundwater, lakes, rivers, and streams. Source water protection is developing and implementing a plan to manage land uses and potential contaminants. To be effective, source water protection should be directed to major threats to the drinking water source identified in the source water assessment. As part of the source water protection plan, a contingency plan for use in the event of an emergency is developed. Source water protection for groundwater is also called wellhead protection. See source water assessment.

Spear point: Generally a shallow bore drilled by simple methods (self-jetted, lowered into augured holes or driven) in unconsolidated sediments for groundwater extraction.

Species: Generally regarded as a group of organisms that resemble each other to a greater degree than members of other groups and that form a reproductively isolated group that will not normally breed with members of another group. (Chemical species are differing compounds of an element.)

Species diversity: An ecological concept that incorporates both the number of species in a particular sampling area and the evenness with which individuals are distributed among the various species.

Species (taxa) richness: The number of species (taxa) present in a defined area or sampling unit.

Specific capacity: The specific capacity of a discharging well at a particular time after discharge commenced is the yield of the well per unit of drawdown at that time. It is not a fixed value. It varies with both the discharge rate and the duration of pumping.

Specific conductance: A measure of the ability of a liquid to conduct an electrical current.

Specific discharge: Also known as Darcian flow velocity. An apparent velocity calculated from Darcy's law; represents the flow rate at which water would flow in an aquifer if the aquifer were an open conduit.

Specific gravity: The weight of a given volume of material compared to the weight of an equal volume of water at a reference temperature under standard conditions.

Specific retention (R): The Specific Retention (R) is the volume retained when the specific yield has been released.

Specific storage (S_s): The volume of water that a unit volume of aquifer releases from or takes into storage under a unit change in hydraulic head.

Specific yield (S_y): The ratio of the volume of water that will drain under the influence of gravity to the volume of saturated rock. It is sometimes referred to as the storage coefficient of an unconfined aquifer.

Spillway volume: Volume at the spillway crest level.

Spit: A small point or low tongue or narrow embankment of land having one end attached to the mainland and the other terminating in open water.

Split sample: A sample prepared by dividing it into two or more equal volumes that each volume is considered a separate sample but representative of the entire sample.

Spoil: Overburden or other waste material removed in mining, quarrying, dredging, or **excavating.**

Spray irrigation: Water is applied to the plant and soil by spraying, usually from pipes with fixed or moving spray nozzles.

Spring: Place where a concentrated discharge of groundwater flows at the ground surface without mechanical aid or via a constructed device such as a bore.

Stage: Height of the water surface above an established datum plane, such as in a river above a predetermined point that may (or may not) be at the channel floor.

Stakeholder: A person or group (e.g. an industry, a government jurisdiction, a community group, the public, etc.) that has an interest or concern in something.

Standard: An objective that is recognised in environmental control laws enforceable by a level of government, for example the water quality standard.

Standard deviation: Statistical measure of the dispersion or scatter of a series of values. It is square root of the variance, which is calculated as the sum of the squares of the deviations from the arithmetic mean, divided by the number of values in the series minus 1.

Standing Water Level (SWL): The depth from ground level (or other stated reference point) to the water level in a bore which is not influenced by pumping. It is expressed as metres.

Static Head: This is the flowing bore equivalent of SWL. It is the height above ground level that water at a particular temperature would stand if the casing were extended upwards. It is expressed as metres or kilopascals.

Static water level (SWL): See standing water level and static head.

Statistics: A branch of mathematics dealing with the collection, analysis and presentation of masses of numerical data.

Stochastic: A description of a parameter or a process with random qualities. A stochastic parameter has a range of possible values, each with a defined probability. The outcome of a stochastic process is not known with certainty.

Storage catchment runoff: The volume of water flowing into storage over a period of time from the catchment between the headwater tributaries and the dam wall and upstream of the storage water surface.

Storage coefficient or storativity (S): The volume of water that a saturated aquifer releases from or takes into storage per unit surface area per unit change of head. It is the product of the specific storage and the aquifer thickness. It can be derived from pumping test analysis and barometric efficiency calculation. It is related to the elastic properties of both the water and the soil matrix. $S = S_s$ x the aquifer thickness.

Storage demand: The volume of water that has been requested to be released from the storage. Note: this may be more than the storage that is actually released.

Storage release: The volume of water released to meet downstream demands. Note: this may be less than storage demand due to release or operational constraints.

Storage reservoir: A natural or artificial impoundment used to hold water before its treatment and/or distribution

Storage spill: The volume of water discharged from the storage in excess of the storage demand.

Storativity: See 'Storage coefficient".

Storm drain: Constructed opening in a road system through which runoff from the road surface flows into an underground system.

Storm surge: An abnormal and sudden rise of sea level along a shore as a result of atmospheric pressure changes and the winds of a storm.

Stormwater: Rainwater that has run off the ground surface, roads, paved areas etc., and is usually carried away by drains.

Strain: A change in the volume or shape of a rock mass in response to stress.

Stratification: A layered structure of sedimentary rocks in which the individual layers can be traced a considerable distance. The layers can be caused by many differences which include materials of different composition, colour, grain size or orientation.

Stratigraphic sequence: The sequence of sedimentary rock layers found in a specific geographic area, arranged in the order of their deposition.

Stratigraphy: The study of sedimentary rock units, including their geographic extent, age, classification, characteristics and formation.

Stratovolcano: A volcanic cone made up of alternating layers of lava flows and pyroclastics. Also known as a composite cone.

Stratum, *pl.* **strata:** A layer within the earth's crust that generally consists of the same kinds of soils or rock material.

Streak: The colour of a mineral in powdered form. Streak is normally determined by scraping a specimen across a surface of unglazed porcelain known as a "streak plate".

Streak Plate: A piece of unglazed porcelain that is used for determining the streak of a mineral specimen.

Stream-aquifer interactions: Relations of water flow and chemistry between streams and aquifers that are hydraulically connected.

Streamfiow: The discharge of water in a natural channel.

Streamline: A line on a map that is parallel to the direction of fluid flow and shows flow patterns. Also lines of fluid flow in a laminar flow situation.

Stream order: A classification system that represents the relative position of streams in a drainage basin. The highest tributaries in the basin are first order streams. These converge to form second order streams, which have only first order streams as their tributaries. Third order streams form by the confluence of two second order streams. The numbering system continues downstream resulting in higher stream orders.

Stream reach: A continuous part of a stream between two specified points.

Stress: A force acting upon or within a mass or rock, expressed in terms of unit weight per surface area such as tons per square inch.

Striations: Scratches or grooves on a rock or sediment surface caused by abrasive action of objects being transported above it by ice, water or wind.

Strike: The geographic direction of a line created by the intersection of a plane and the horizontal. Often used to describe the geographic "trend" of a fold or fault.

Strike-slip fault: A fault with horizontal displacement, typically caused by shear stress.

Stromatolite: A mound-shaped fossil that forms from the repetitious layering of algal mat covered by trapped sediment particles.

Strombolian eruption: A type of volcanic eruption characterized by fountains of lava jetting from a lava-filled central crater.

Stygofauna: Any fauna that live within groundwater systems, such as caves and aquifers, or more specifically small, aquatic groundwater invertebrates.

Subartesian: Groundwater that does not rise above the surface of the ground when accessed by a bore and must be pumped to the surface.

Subartesian bore: A bore in which the standing water level is below ground level.

Subartesian water: A confined aquifer containing groundwater that will, if tapped by a bore, not flow naturally to the surface.

Subduction Zone: An area at a convergent plate boundary where an oceanic plate is being forced down into the mantle beneath another plate. These can be identified by a zone of progressively deeper earthquakes.

Sublimation: The transition of a substance from the solid phase directly to the vapour phase, or vice versa, without passing through an intermediate liquid phase.

Submerged plant: A plant that lies entirely beneath the water surface, except for flowering parts of some species.

Submarine canyon: An underwater canyon, carved into the continental shelf. These can be carved by turbidity currents or carved subaerially during a time when sea level was lower.

Subsidence: The gradual downward settling or sinking of the Earth's surface with little or no horizontal motion.

Substrate: A layer of material beneath the surface soil. Also, the surface beneath a wetland, lake, or stream in which organisms grow or to which organisms are attached.

Subsurface drain: A shallow drain installed to intercept the rising groundwater level and maintain the water table at an acceptable depth below the land surface.

Subtidal: Continuously submerged; an area affected by ocean tides.

Subtropical anticyclone: A semipermanent anticyclone located, on the average, over oceans near 30^0 N. and 30^0 S. latitude.

Supercontinent: A large landmass that forms from the convergence of multiple continents.

Superficial aquifer: is the aquifer nearest the surface, having no overlying confining layer. The upper surface of the groundwater within the aquifer is called the watertable. See also unconfined aquifer and surficial aquifer.

Superposed stream: A stream that cuts across resistant **bedrock** units. This can occur when the stream's course was determined at a previous time and on a previous landscape.

Superposition: The concept that the oldest rock layers are at the bottom of a sequence with younger rock layers deposited on top of them. This can be considered a rule that applies in all situations, except where the rocks are extremely deformed.

Supersaturated solution: A solution that contains more solute than its solubility allows. Such a solution is unstable and precipitation can be triggered by a variety of events.

Supply network: A distribution supply network of carriers which is used to convey water either under gravity or pressurised, from a source, typically a regulated river network, through customer service points to customer properties. A supply network may also be described as being an irrigation or non-irrigation (domestic and stock) network depending on the predominant purpose for which customers use the water supplied through the network.

Supply pipeline: Closed conduit designed to convey way under pressure from upstream source to farms. Supply pipelines are categorised as:

Main pipelines: whose primary purpose is to deliver water from storage or river into the distribution system

Rising mains: particular forms of main pipeline that convey water directly from a pump to a higher elevation (often storage)

Distribution pipelines: whose primary purpose is to deliver water from main channels or pipelines to individual farms

High pressure systems: where the deliver pressure is sufficient to operate pressurised on-farm irrigation systems

Low pressure systems: where the deliver pressure is usually sufficient to allow flood or furrow irrigation and additional pumping is required on farm to operate pressurised irrigation.

Surf: The breaking of waves as they enter shallow water.

Surf Zone: An area of breaking waves bounded by the point of first breakers, then landward to the maximum uprush of waves on the beach.

Surface drainage system: System of open drainage channels, modified natural waterways and/or storages designed to collect drainage from rainfall and irrigation runoff on rural lands and convey it to disposal.

Surface inflow: Water flowing on the surface into an entity from adjoining entities. Includes river flows and overbank flows.

Surface outflow: Water flowing on the surface out of an entity from adjoining entities. Includes river flows and overbank flows.

Surface runoff: Runoff that travels over the land surface to the nearest stream channel.

Surface water: Water above the surface of the land, including lakes, rivers, streams, ponds, floodwater, and runoff.

Surface water diversion service: A rural water service that provides for the diversion of raw water by customers from a surface water source at a specified level of service and which confers common obligations on customers. Typically, service provision involves water access, works or site licence administration, metering or measurement and monitoring of diversions on a regular basis. Aspects of water planning and water resource management may also be involved. Surface diversion services are classified into three sub-categories:

Regulated surface diversion service: A service that enables customers to pump or divert from a surface water source, typically a river that is regulated or controlled by a structure or structures operated by a rural water delivery agency.

Drainage diversion: A service that enables customers to pump or divert from a surface drain operated by a rural water delivery agency. In some circumstances, drainage diversion is included in the surface drainage service and the reporting agency should report against the primary service with explanatory comment provided.

Unregulated surface diversion service: A service that enables customers to pump or divert under specified conditions from a surface water source, typically a stream, that is not regulated or controlled by a structure or structures operated by a rural water delivery agency.

Surface wave: A type of seismic wave that travels along Earth's surface.

Surficial (superficial) aquifers: These occur in alluvial sediments in river valleys, deltas, basins and coastal plains, in lake or lacustrine sediments, and in *aeolian* or wind-formed deposits. They are essentially unconsolidated day, silt, sand, gravel, and limestone formations, mainly of Quaternary age (under 1.8 million years). These deposits are easily exploited and are the major sources of freshwater groundwater when associated with larger river systems.

Survey: Sampling of a representative number of sites during a given hydrologic condition.

Suspended: (As used in tables of chemical analyses), the amount (concentration) of undissolved material in a water- sediment mixture. Most commonly refer to that material retained on a 0.45 pm filter.

Suspended load: Small particles being carried by a stream and held in suspension by the movement of the water.

Suspended sediment: Sediment that is transported in suspension by a stream.

Suspended solids: Different from suspended sediment only in the way that the sample is collected and analysed.

Suspended-sediment concentration: The velocity-weighted concentration of suspended sediment in the sampled zone (from the water surface to a point approximately 0.1m above the bed); expressed as milligrams of dry sediment per litre of water-sediment mixture (mglL).

Suspension: Transport of sediment by wind or water currents that are strong enough to keep the sediment particles continuously above the stream bottom or ground

Sustainable yield: The amount of water that can be taken annually by all users (economic, social and environmental) from a source of supply over a period of years without depleting that source beyond its ability to be replenished naturally in "wet years." A proposed national definition is "The extraction regime, measured over a specified planning timeframe that allows acceptable levels of stress and protects the higher value issues (economic, social and environmental) that have a dependency on the water.

Swale: A slight depression sometimes filled with water, in the midst of generally level land.

Swamp: An area intermittently or permanently covered with water, and having trees and shrubs.

SWRO: Sea water reverse osmosis

Symbiosis: A relationship between two species who live in close association but do not compete with each other or prey on one another. At least one of the species derives benefit from this association.

Syncline: A fold in the earth's crust, concave upwards, whose core contains stratigraphically younger rocks.

Synoptic sites: Sites sampled during a short-term investigation of specific water-quality conditions during selected seasonal or hydrologic conditions, to provide improved spatial resolution for critical water quality conditions.

System: A stratigraphic unit of major significance which was deposited during a specific time period, and which can be correlated worldwide on the basis of its fossil content.

T

Tableland: An area of elevated land with a nearly level surface.

TABS-MD: A suite of 2D hydrodynamic software including flow and transport models developed by the US Army Corps of Engineers including GFGEN, RMA2 and RMA4.

Take: To remove water from, or to reduce the flow of water in or into, the water resource including by any of the following means:

Pumping or siphoning water from the water resource;

Stopping, impeding or diverting the flow of water in or into the water resource;

Releasing water from the water resource is the water resource is a wetland or lake;

Permitting water to flow from the resource if the water resource is a well or watercourse.

Tailings: Rock that remains after processing ore to remove the valuable minerals.

Tailwater: Flow of surface water from a given area resulting from the effects of applied irrigation water in excess or crop water requirement and leaching. Talus

Talus: An accumulation of angular rock debris at the base of a cliff or steep slope that was produced by physical weathering.

Target criteria: Quantitative or qualitative parameters established for preventive measures to indicate performance; performance goals.

Target formation: The intended geological formation or production zone.

Tar sand: A sandstone that contains asphalt within its pore spaces.

Tarn: A relatively small and deep, steep-sided lake or pool occupying an ice-gouged basin amid glaciated mountains.

Taxa richness: See Species richness.

Taxon (plural taxa): Any identifiable group of taxonomically related organisms.

TCF: Trillion cubic feet (of natural gas)

Tectonic activity: Movement of the Earth's crust resulting in the formation of ocean basins, continents, plateaux, and mountain ranges.

Tectonics: The study of processes that move and deform Earth's crust.

Telemetry: A technology which allows remote measurement and reporting of information collected at wells, compressor stations and gas pipeline valves and meters.

Telescoping: A method of fitting or placing one casing inside another or introducing a screen through a casing diameter larger than the diameter of the screen.

Temporary wetland: A type of wetland in which water is present for only part of the year, usually during wet or rainy seasons; also known as vernal pools.

Tenement: The area and location over which an ATP is granted.

Terminal moraine: The end moraine extending across a glacial plain or valley as an accurate or crescent ridge that marks the farthest advance or maximum extent of a glacier.

Terminal seepage rate: The constant rate of seepage attained once the groundwater mound caused by the channel seepage rises to the elevation of the water surface in the channel.

Terrestrial: Pertaining to, consisting of, or representing the Earth.

Terrestrial planet: One of the four rocky planets closest to the sun, which include Mars, Venus, Earth and Mercury.

Terrigenous sediment: Sediment that is derived from the weathering of rocks which are exposed above sea level.

Tertiary-treated sewage: Principally designed to remove nutrients, such as phosphorus (typically 95%) are also removed. Tertiary treatment may additionally target other contaminants of concern like toxicants and salt. Typical tertiary sewage treatment processes may include biological nutrient removal plants, chemical dosing of secondary plants for nutrient removal (including lagoons), enhanced pond treatment systems for nutrient removal, reverse osmosis and advanced filtration systems, membrane bioreactors and secondary treatment plus grass plots or wetlands for nutrient removal.

Tertiary treatment: Included treatment processes beyond secondary or biological processes, which further improve effluent quality. Tertiary treatment processes include detention in lagoons, conventional filtration via sand, dual media or membrane filters, which may include coagulant dosing and land-based or wetland processes.

Test bore/well: A borehole drilled to test an aquifer by means of pumping tests.

Test hole: A hole used only to obtain information on groundwater quality and/or geological and hydrological conditions.

Texture: The visible characteristics of a rock which include its grain size, grain orientation, rounding, angularity or presence of vesicles.

TCF or Tcf: Trillion cubic feet (1000 cubic feet).

Theis equation: An equation for the unsteady flow of groundwater in a fully confined aquifer to a pumping well.

Thermal loading: Amount of waste heat discharged to a water body.

Thermal Pollution: Water quality is not defined by chemistry alone. If natural waters are withdrawn for use they should be returned to the environment at approximately the same temperature. An increase or decrease in temperature can have an adverse effect upon plants, animals and chemical balances. Returning water to a stream at a different temperature than it was withdrawn is known as thermal pollution. For example, coal-fired power plants use water in the production of steam that turns turbines. That water is then cooled in the large cooling towers before it is returned to the environment.

Thermal spring: Heated groundwater that naturally flows to the land surface.

Thermoelectric power: Electrical power generated by use of fossil-fuel, oil or natural gas, geothermal, or nuclear energy.

Thixotropy: The property exhibited by certain gels of becoming fluid when stirred or shaken and returning to the semi solid state upon standing.

Threaded PVC: A type of PVC that has male and female threads on each end, which gives a flush inside and outside joint, avoiding the need for solvents. A sealant or flexible sealant is recommended to ensure the joints are watertight. The use of solvents for this purpose is not recommended.

Tidal Current: Currents of water that are produced in response to a rising or falling tide. These currents can flow into or out of a bay, delivering the rising water or removing the falling water.

Tidal flat: An extensive, nearly horizontal, tract of land that is alternately covered and uncovered by the tide and consists of unconsolidated sediment.

Tidal efficiency: A measure of the incompetence of the confining beds of a confined aquifer to resist changes in pressure resulting from ocean tides and from earth tides. This incompetence results in water level changes in a confined aquifer.

Tidal wave: A term that is incorrectly used in reference to a tsunami. Tsunamis have nothing to do with the tides.

Tide: The rhythmic, alternate rise and fall of the water level of the ocean, and connected bodies of water, occurring twice a day over most of the Earth, resulting from the gravitational attraction of the Moon, and to a lesser degree, the Sun.

Tile drain: A buried perforated box designed to remove excess water from soils.

Till: Predominantly unsorted and un-stratified drift, deposited directly by and underneath a glacier without subsequent reworking by melt water, and consisting of a heterogeneous mixture of clay, silt, sand, gravel, and boulders.

Time of concentration: The longest time it takes for a particle of water to travel to the watershed outlet in a given watershed.

TIN: Triangulated Irregular Network

Title: A licence issued by the State to grant a company exclusive rights to explore or mine minerals and petroleum within a defined area. A title (tenement) will only be granted once a company has demonstrated that the resource is of benefit to the State and can be extracted safely without endangering people, the environment or heritage and infrastructure.

TJ: Terajoule (10^{12} joules)

Tolerant species: Those species that are adaptable to (tolerant of) human alterations to the environment and often increase in number when alterations occur.

Topographic divide: The boundary between adjacent surface water boundaries. It is represented by a topographically high area.

Topographic map: A map that shows the change in elevation over a geographic area through the use of contour lines. The contour lines trace points of equal elevation across the map.

Topography: The general configuration of a land surface or any part of the Earth's surface, including its relief and the position of its natural and man-made features.

Tortuosity: The actual length of a groundwater flow path, which is sinuous in form, divided by the straight-line distance between the ends of the flow path.

Total available water: The volume of water in a soil that can be utilised by plant roots. It is the amount of water released between in-situ field capacity and the permanent wilting point.

Total concentration: Refers to the concentration of a constituent regardless of its form (dissolved or bound) in a sample.

Total dissolved solids (TDS): Total dissolved solids consist of inorganic salts and small amounts of organic matter that are dissolved in water. Clay particles, colloidal iron and manganese oxides, and silica fine enough to pass through a 0.45 micrometer filer membrane can also contribute to total dissolved solids. Total dissolved solids comprise sodium, potassium, calcium, magnesium, chloride, sulphate, bicarbonate, carbonate, silica, organic matter, fluoride, iron, manganese, nitrate (and nitrite) and phosphate (NHMRC & NRMMC 2004a).

Total head (or hydraulic head): The height above a datum plane of a column of water. In a groundwater system, it is composed of elevation head and pressure head.

Total net flows: Total surface water runoff and deep drainage to groundwater (groundwater recharge) and transfers into the water system (both surface and groundwater), for a defined area.

Total quality management: Adds to the concepts of quality management a long-term global management strategy and the participation of all members of the organisation for the benefit of the organisation itself, its members, its customers and society as a whole.

Total water resource: Total inflows to surface and groundwater in a giver year, for a defined area, plus the net volume of water in stare at the start of the year.

Toxicant: An element or compound with a harmful or lethal effect on the physiology, behaviour, reproduction or survival of an organism.

Toxicity: The extent to which a compound is is capable of causing injury or death, especially by chemical means.

Toxicology: Study of poisons, their effects, antidotes and detection.

Trace element: A chemical element that is present in minute quantities in a substance.

Tracer: A stable, easily detected substance or a radio isotope added to a material to follow the location of the substance in the environment or to detect any physical or chemical changes that it undergoes.

Trachyte: A fine-grained volcanic rock that contains large amounts of potassium feldspar.

Traction: Transport of sediment by wind or water in which the sediment remains in contact with the ground or bed of the stream, moving by rolling or sliding

Trade winds: A prevailing pattern of easterly winds that dominate most of the tropics. A major component of the general circulation of the atmosphere.

Transgression: An advance of the sea over land areas. Possible causes include a rise in sea level or subsidence.

Transmissivity (Coefficient of transmissivity): A measure of the capability of the entire thickness of an aquifer to transmit water. It is defined as the rate of flow of fluid through a unit width of aquifer, normal to the direction of flow, under a unit gradient. It is the product of hydraulic conductivity and aquifer thickness.

Transpire: To emit or give off water vapour through the surface, as of the body, of leaves etc.

Transpiration: The process by which water absorbed by plants (usually through the roots) is evaporated into the atmosphere from the plant surface (principally from the leaves).

Transverse Dunes: Sand dunes that are oriented at right angles to the direction of the prevailing wind. These form where vegetation is sparse and the sand supply is abundant.

Trap: A sedimentary or tectonic structure where oil and/or natural gas has accumulated. These are structural highs where a porous rock unit is capped by an impermeable rock unit. Oil and gas trapped within the porous rock unit migrate to a high point in the structure because of their low density.

Travertine: Calcium carbonate deposits which form in caves and around hot springs where carbonate-bearing waters are exposed to the air. The water evaporates, leaving a small deposit of calcium carbonate.

Treated CSG water: This is CSG water that undergone a process to remove or reduce contaminants to make the water suitable for a desired end use.

Treated effluent discharge: Where wastewater treatment plant effluent is not reused, the treated effluent may be disposed to land, evaporative ponds, rivers and other streams or the ocean. For the purposes of the water balance, we are interested only in treated effluent discharged back to rivers and other streams.

Treatment: Application of techniques such as settlement, filtration and chlorination to render water suitable for specific purposes, including drinking and discharge to the environment.

Trellis drainage: A drainage pattern in which streams intersect at right angles. This forms in areas of long parallel valleys such as in folded mountain belts. Rivers occupy the valleys and tributary streams join them at right angles.

Tremie pipe: A device or small-diameter pipe that carries materials to a designated depth in the hole

Trench: A long, narrow, deep depression in the ocean floor that parallels a convergent boundary involving at least one oceanic plate.

Triazine herbicide: A class of herbicides containing a symmetrical triazine ring (a nitrogen-heterocyclic ring composed of three nitrogens and three carbons in an alternating sequence). Examples include atrazine, propazine, and simazine.

Triazine pesticide: See Triazine herbicide.

Tributary: A river or stream flowing into a larger river, stream or lake.

Tributary inflow: The volume of water flowing into the headwaters of the storage over a period of time.

Triple junction: A point where three lithospheric plates meet. Triple junctions can be areas of unusual tectonic activity due to the differential motions of the three intersecting plates.

Tritium: A radioactive form of hydrogen with atoms of three times the mass of ordinary hydrogen; can be used to determine the age of water

Tropical cyclone: A tropical cyclone is a storm system characterized by a large low-pressure centre and numerous thunderstorms that produce strong winds and heavy rain. They originate over the tropical oceans and are fuelled by high ocean temperatures and the rotation is caused by Coriolis force. Tropical cyclones are classified according to their intensity and windspeed. Their rotation is clockwise in the southern hemisphere and anticlockwise in the northern hemisphere. They are also called hurricanes and typhoons in the northern hemisphere. See also Cyclone.

Troposphere: Lowest 6 to 12 miles of the atmosphere, characterized by a general decrease in temperature with height, appreciable water content, and active weather processes.

Trough (groundwater): An elongated depression in a potentiometric surface.

Trough (meteorological): An elongated area of relatively low atmospheric pressure; the opposite of a ridge. This term commonly is used to distinguish a feature from the closed circulation of a low (or cyclone). A large trough, however, may include one or more lows, and an upper-air trough may be associated with a lower-level low.

True colour units: True colour units are a measure of degree of colour in water.

Tsunami: A large sea wave normally produced by sudden movement of the ocean floor caused by an earthquake or volcanic eruption. These waves can travel at high speeds across an ocean basin and cause great destruction when they reach land.

Tube drain: Buried horizontal pipeline containing openings (or slots) to allow gravity entry of excess groundwater which is then led to a suitable point of discharge or pit. A tube drain system can include linings constructed from joined slotted plastic pipes or terracotta pipes laid end to end (referred to as a "tile drain").

Turbidite: A vertical sequence of sediments deposited by a turbidity current. Because the largest particles of the current settle first a turbidite will be graded deposits with coarsest grain sizes at the bottom and finer grain sizes going upwards.

Turbidity: The cloudiness or haziness of water caused by the presence of fine suspended matter.

Turbidity Current: A mixture of sediment particles and water that flows down the continental slope. These high density currents can reach great speeds and generally erode loose sediments from the seafloor beneath them.

Turbulent flow: Flow in which the fluid particles move in a haphazard manner rather than in parallel paths or streamlines.

Two pass: A second stage in the reverse osmosis system that enables a high recovery to occur.

U

UCG: Underground Coal Gasification

UCTL: Underground Coal Conversion to Liquids

Ultrabasic rock: An igneous rock with a very low silica content and rich in minerals such as hypersthene, augite and olivine. These rocks are also known as ultramafic rocks.

Ultra-filtration: Enables removal of particles within 0.001 – 0.01 micron range through the use of a mircoporous membrane.

Uncertainty analysis: The quantification of uncertainty in model results due to incomplete knowledge of model aquifer parameters, boundary conditions or stresses.

Unconfined aquifer: A permeable formation only partly filled with water and overlying a relatively impervious zone. It contains water which is not subjected to any pressure other than its own weight. If a bore penetrates such an aquifer the water will rise up the bore no higher than the level at which it was encountered.

Unconformity: A contact between two rock units of significantly different ages. An unconformity is a gap in the time record for that location.

Unconsolidated deposit: Deposit of loosely bound sediment that typically fills topographically low areas.

Unconsolidated rock: Loosely bound geologic formation composed of sands and gravel.

Unconsolidated formation: Loose, soft rock-material strata of sedimentary, igneous or metamorphic-type rock, which includes sand, gravel and mixtures of sand and gravel. These formations are widely distributed and can possess good storage and water transmissivity characteristics.

Unconventional gas: Natural gases which occur in less permeable sources. These include coal seam gas extracted from coal deposits, shale gas extracted from shale and tight gas, which is extracted from lowers of low-permeability rock.

Understory: A foliage layer lying beneath and shaded by the main canopy of a forest.

Uniformity coefficient: The ratio of the D_{60} and the D_{10} in a granular sample. Where, D_{60} and D_{10} are the grain size diameters of particles in a sample such that 60% and 10% respectively of particles in the sample are finer.

Uniformitarianism: A basic geologic principle. Processes that act upon the Earth today are the same processes that have acted upon it in the past. The present is the key to the past.

Unit Cell: The smallest sample of a substance that has a complete representation of its atomic structure. A crystal structure is formed by repetition of the unit cell in three dimensions.

Unit Hydrograph: A runoff hydrograph that represents the volume of runoff for a unit depth of water applied to the entire watershed. For specific watersheds, a unit hydrograph developed for a given amount of runoff can be used to generate hydrographs of differing runoff amounts for storms with the same duration.

Unregulated system: River system where flows are not regulated by the operation of structures such as major dams or weirs.

Unsaturated zone: (See aeration zone). A subsurface zone above the water table in which the pore spaces may contain a combination of air and water.

Upgradient: Of or pertaining to the place(s) from which groundwater originated or travelled through before reaching a given point in an aquifer.

Upland: A general term for non wetland; elevated land above low areas along streams or between hills; any elevated region from which rivers gather drainage.

Uplift: A structurally high area in Earth's crust. Formed by movements that bend the crust into a structure such as a dome or an arch.

Upstream regulation: A method of channel regulation where the water level being controlled or maintained is upstream of the control point. Most manually controlled systems in Australia are designed on this basis. Drop bars are removed or placed, or opened or closed to maintain a steady level upstream of a regulating point.

Upwelling: Movement of cold water from the floor of a lake or ocean up into a shallow area.

Uranium (U): A heavy silvery-white metallic element, highly radioactive and easily oxidized. Of the 14 known isotopes of uranium, U_{238} is the most abundant in nature.

Urban diversions: The volume of water extracted from waterways to supply towns and does not include water for stock and domestic use. The volume of urban diversions is the total volume of water diverted and includes any losses in the distribution system.

Urban site: A site that has greater than 50 percent urbanised and less than 25 percent agricultural area.

U-shaped Valley: A deep valley with a flat floor and very steep walls. Shaped in cross-section like the letter "U". Valleys with this geometry are frequently cut by a glacier.

V

Vadose water: Water that exists in the pore spaces of a rock or soil, between the ground surface and the water table.

Vadose zone: See Unsaturated zone.

Valence electrons: Electrons in the outermost shell of an atom. The electrons that are typically involved in making chemical bonds.

Validation: See Verification.

Validation of processes: The substantiation by scientific evidence (investigative or experimental studies) of existing or new processes and the operational criteria to ensure capability to effectively control hazards.

Valley Glacier: A glacier that occurs in a mountainous region and occupies a valley. Also known as an Alpine Glacier.

Van der Waals Bond: A weak chemical bond in which atoms are held together by weak electrostatic attraction.

Vapour: The state of water in the hydrologic cycle in which individual molecules are highly energized and move about freely; also known as gas/gaseous.

Varve: A thin layer of fine-grained sediment deposited in the still waters of a lake. Varves are frequently associated with glaciation and represent a yearly sedimentation cycle - a silty, light-coloured layer deposited in summer and a darker, organic-rich clay layer deposited during winter.

Vascular plant: A plant composed of or provided with vessels or ducts that convey water or sap. A fern is an example of this type of plant.

Vector data: Digital data comprised of points, lines, and polygons.

Vein: A fracture that has been filled with mineral material.

Ventifact: A rock that has been shaped or polished by the sandblasting effect of wind-blown sand.

Verification: A test of the integrity of a model by checking if its predictions reasonably match the observations of a reserved data set, deliberately excluded from consideration during calibration.

Verification of drinking water quality: An assessment of the overall performance of the water supply system and the ultimate quality of drinking water being supplied to consumers; incorporated both drinking water quality monitoring and monitoring of consumer satisfaction.

Vernal pool: A small lake or pond that is filled with eater for only a short time during the spring.

Vesicle: Spherical or elongated cavities in an igneous rock that are created when a melt crystallizes with bubbles of gas trapped inside.

Virus: Molecules of nucleic acid (RNA or DNA) that can enter cells and replicate in them.

Viscosity: The property of fluid describing its resistance to flow. Units of viscosity are Newton-seconds per metre squared or Pascal-seconds. Viscosity is also known as dynamic viscosity.

Voids ratio: The ratio of the volume of voids to the volume of solids in a soil sample.

Volatile organic compounds (VOCS): Organic chemicals that have a high vapour pressure relative to their water solubility. VOCs include components of gasoline, fuel oils and lubricants as well as organic solvents fumigants some inert ingredients in pesticides and some by-products of chlorine disinfection.

Volatization: To become or make volatile; to evaporate or cause to evaporate.

Volcanic ash: Sand-sized particles of igneous rock that form when a spray of liquid magma is blown from a volcanic vent by escaping gas.

Volcanic ash fall: An accumulation of volcanic ash produced by an eruption. These can be very thick near the vent and decrease to a light dusting in a downwind direction.

Volcanic bomb: A projectile of hot magma or rock that is blown from the vent during a volcanic eruption. These solidify in flight and frequently form an elongated rock of streamlined shape.

Volcanic breccia: A rock made up of pyroclastic fragments that are at least 64 millimetres in diameter.

Volcanic cone: A cone-shaped hill or mountain composed of pyroclastic debris and/or lava which builds up around a volcanic vent during eruptions.

Volcanic dome: A steep-sided extrusion of very viscous lava that is squeezed from a volcanic vent without major eruption. These are frequently rhyolitic in composition and produce a rounded mound above the vent.

Volcanic neck: A vertical intrusion with the geometry of a volcanic pipe. An erosional remant of a volcanic pipe.

Volcanic pipe: A vertical or nearly vertical tunnel which connects a magma reservoir to the surface. Magma and gas travel up this tube to produce the eruption. After the eruption the tube can be filled with a cooling magma which preserves its shape as an intrusive body.

Volcano: A vent in Earth's surface through which molten rock and gases escape. The term also refers to deposits of ash and lava which accumulate around this vent.

V-shaped valley: A valley with a narrow bottom and a cross section shaped like the letter "V". Valleys of this shape are almost always cut by stream erosion.

W

W or Watt: Power which in one second give rise to energy of one joule.

Wadi: A stream valley in an arid region that is dry except during the rainy season.

Wall cake: A low permeability film that is deposited on the porous face of the borehole by the drilling fluid to prevent fluid loss (the ability to deposit this film is a principal requirement of the drilling fluid).

Wall cake thickness: The thickness of the wall cake that has been deposited on the porous face of the borehole by the drilling fluid.

Warping: A slight bend, uplift or subsidence of Earth's crust on a regional scale.

Wastewater: Water that has been used for some purpose and would normally be treated and discarded. Wastewater usually contains significant quantities of pollutant. This could be water that is discharged to sewers or other collection points following its use in households or during industrial processes. Water collected during mining or oil and gas extraction processes is also referred to as wastewater. There is a growing emphasis on treating wastewater to enable its reuse.

Wastewater treatment: Any of the mechanical or chemical processes used to modify the quality of wastewater in order to make it more compatible or acceptable to humans and the environment.

Wasteway: A waterway used to drain excess irrigation water dumped from the irrigation delivery system.

Water (H_2O): An odourless, tasteless, colourless liquid made up of a combination of hydrogen and oxygen. Water forms streams, lakes, and seas, and is a major constituent of all living matter.

Water allocation: The specific volume of water allocated to water access entitlements in a given season.

Water-bearing rocks: Several types of rocks can hold water, including: sedimentary deposits (sand and gravel), channels in carbonate rocks (limestone), lava tubes or cooling fractures in igneous rocks, and fractures in hard rocks.

Water budget: An accounting of the inflow to, outflow from, and storage changes of water in a hydrologic unit.

Water column: An imaginary straight column extending through a water body from its floor to its surface.

Water content of snow: Amount of liquid water in the snow at the time of observation; water equivalent of snow.

Water cycle: The movement of water between the atmosphere, ground and surface water bodies through the processes of evaporation, precipitation, infiltration, percolation, transpiration and runoff. Also known as the "hydrologic cycle".

Water demand: Water requirements for a particular purpose, such as irrigation, power, municipal supply, plant transpiration, or storage.

Water exports: Artificial transfer (by pipes or canals) of freshwater from one region or subregion to another.

Water imports: Artificial transfer (by pipes or canals) of freshwater to one region or subregion from another.

Water purification: The removal of undesirable materials and contaminants from source water to improve quality to a standard that makes the water suitable for specific purposes, for example: potable use, food processing and mineral processing.

Water quality: Water quality is the collective term for the physical, aesthetic, chemical and biological properties of water.

Water-quality criteria: Specific levels of water quality which, if reached, are expected to render a body of water unsuitable for its designated use.

Water-quality guidelines: Specific levels of water quality which, if reached, may adversely affect human health or aquatic life.

Water resource: Surface water or groundwater; or a watercourse, lake, wetland or aquifer (whether or not currently has water in it); and includes all aspects of the water resource (including water, organisms and other components and ecosystems that contribute to the physical stage and environmental value of the water resource).

Water rights: Legal rights to the use of water. See also Riparian rights.

Water stock: Surface and groundwater resources available in Australia for economic and environmental use.

Water supply: The system of dams, pipes, etc., by which water is supplied to a community or region.

Water system: A system that is hydrologically connected and described at the level desired for management purposes (e.g. sub-catchment, catchment, basin, aquifer, groundwater basin, etc.).

Water table: The potentiometric level in an unconfined aquifer. The upper level of the unconfined groundwater, where the water pressure is equal to that of the atmosphere and below which the soils or rocks are saturated. It is the location where the sub-surface becomes fully saturated with groundwater, the level at which water stands in wells that penetrate the water body. Above the water table, the sub-surface is only partially saturated (often called the unsaturated zone). The water table can be measured by installing shallow wells extending just into the zone of saturation and then measuring the water level in those wells.

Water treatment: The generic term describing the many and varied processes used to make water suitable for specific purposes. Examples range from filtration of fresh water to remove sediments and make it suitable for potable use, to complex reverse osmosis processes allied without treatments to remove salts and other contaminants. Apart from desalination, such processes are often used to treat wastewater making it suitable for reuse for irrigation, environmental and industrial purposes.

Water treatment plant: A facility that treats water to remove contaminants so that it can be safely used.

Water use: The volume of water diverted from a stream or extracted from groundwater or transferred to another area for use. It is not representative of the on farm or town use, but is representative of the volume taken from the environment.

Water vapour: Gaseous water, especially when diffused and below the boiling point, distinguished from steam.

Water well: Any hole excavated in the ground that can be used to obtain a water supply. In Australia the term "well" is commonly replaced by "bore" and "well" refers to a larger diameter facility.

Water year: A continuous 12-month period selected to present data relative to hydrologic or meteorological phenomena during which a complete annual hydrologic cycle normally occurs. The period selected for a water year can vary from place to place even in one country.

Water-on-demand: A type of network supply or regulated surface diversion service where customers are permitted an able to take water from a supply service at any time without ordering during the normal operation period. This service supply mode may be subject to occasional restrictions or rostering as a result of shortages in supply availability.

Watercourse: A river, creek or other natural watercourse (whether modified or not), in which water is contained or flows (whether permanently or from time to time).

Waterfall: A steep fall or flow of water from a height; a cascade.

Waterhole: A natural hole or hollow in which water collects, as a spring in a desert, a cavity in the dried-up course of a river, etc.

Waterlogging: Process of soil becoming saturated with water, generally for an extended period.

Waterproof: Impervious to water.

Water recycling: A generic term for water reclamation and reuse. It can also be used to describe a specific type of 'reuse' where water is recycled and used again for the same purpose (e.g. recirculating systems for washing and cooling), with or without treatment in between.

Watershed: The land area from which surface runoff drains into a stream, channel, lake, reservoir, or other body of water; also called a drainage basin.

Watertable: Groundwater in proximity of the soil surface with no confining layers between the groundwater and soil surface.

Waterway: A river, canal, or other body of water as a route or way of travel or transport.

Wave: A movement of the surface of a liquid body, such as sea or lake, in the form of a ridge or a swell.

Wave-Cut Terrace: A long, level surface formed by wave erosion during a time when sea level was higher.

Wavelength: An interval of repetition in a wave-like disturbance. The distance between two successive crests or two successive troughs.

Weather: State of the atmosphere at any particular time and place.

Weathering: Process whereby earthy or rocky materials are changed in colour, texture, composition, or form (with little or no transportation) by exposure to atmospheric agents.

Weighted mean: A value obtained by multiplying each of a series of values by its assigned weight, and dividing the sum of these products by the sum of the weights. In the ordinary arithmetic mean, each value is assigned a weight of 1.

Weir: A structure on a river to facilitate regulation of flow or diversion to storages or supply networks.

Well: A bored, drilled or driven shaft, or a dug hole whose depth is greater than the largest surface dimension and whose purpose is to reach groundwater supplies to inject, extract or monitor water. Also called a bore.

Well casing: Steel lining used to provide the structural basis for a gas well or core hole.

Well closure: The process of sealing a well that is no longer being used to prevent groundwater contamination and harm to people and animals.

Well development: The process whereby a well is pumped or surged to remove any fine material that may be blocking the well screen or the aquifer outside the well screen.

Well efficiency: The ratio of idealised drawdown in the well, where there are no losses resulting from well design and construction factors, to actual measured drawdown in the well.

Well, fully penetrating: A well drilled to the bottom of an aquifer, constructed in such a way that it withdraws water from the entire thickness of the aquifer.

Well, partially penetrating: A well constructed in such a way that it draws water directly from a fractional part of the total thickness of the aquifer. The fractional part may be located at the top or bottom or anywhere in between in the aquifer.

Well field/Bore field: An area in which productive wells/bores are drilled.

Well screen: A tubular device with either slots, holes, gauze, or continuous-wire wrap; used at the end of a well casing to complete a well. The water enters the well through the well screen.

Well siting: Location of a well/bore placed to best protect water quality, access adequate water quantity, and allow for inspection and maintenance of the facility.

Wellhead protection zones (WHPZs): They are generally circular (unless information is available to determine a different shape or size), with a 500m radius around each production bore in a P1 area and a 300m radius around each production bore in P2 and P3 areas. WHPZs do not extend outside the boundary of the water reserve.

Wetland function: A process or series of processes that take place within a wetland that are beneficial to the wetland itself, the surrounding ecosystems, and people.

Wetlands: Lands where water saturation is the dominant factor in determining the nature of soil development and the types of plant and animal communities. Other common names for wetlands are sloughs, ponds, and marshes.

Withdrawal: Water removed from a surface or groundwater source for use.

WMS: Watershed Modelling System

Wonky holes: Submarine freshwater springs in the seabed.

X

Xenoblast: A crystal that has grown in a rock during the process of metamorphism and which has not developed its characteristic crystal faces because of space limitations.

Xenolith: A preexisting rock that has been incorporated into magma without melting. When the magma crystallizes the preexisting rock fragment is known as a xenolith.

Xerophyte: A plant that can survive in a very dry location or climate.

X-ray diffraction: A technique used to identify minerals by bombarding them with X-rays. Planes of repetition within the atomic structure of the mineral diffract the X-rays. The pattern of diffraction is unique for each mineral structure and can be used for identification.

Y

Yazoo stream: A tributary that parallels the main channel for a considerable distance. Joining of these streams is normally blocked by a natural levee along the larger stream.

Yellow ground: Oxidized kimberlite. A yellow soil that is characteristic of the area above a kimberlite diamond pipe.

Yield: The mass of material or constituent transported by a river in a specified period of time divided by the drainage areas of the river basin. Also, the long term sustainable supply from a bore or a groundwater system.

Youth: The earliest stage in the development of a landscape. During this stage streams are actively downcutting and flowing straight for long distances with frequent waterfalls and rapids. The valleys are typically steep sided and v-shaped.

Z

Zeolite: A group of hydrous aluminosilicates that are similar to the feldspars. They easily lose and regain their water of hydration and they fuse and swell when heated. Zeolites are frequently used in water softening, ion exchange and absorbent applications.

Zinc blende: A term used in reference to the mineral sphalerite.

Zirconium: A mineral, zirconium silicate. A hard mineral with a high index of refraction that is used as a gemstone and as an ore of zirconium.

Zoned crystal: A crystal that grew while temperatures were changing or while the composition of the parent solution was changing. Crystals of these minerals can have a range of compositions, with a certain chemistry in the centre reflecting the early growth conditions and the outer chemistry reflecting the later growth conditions. Minerals such as olivine or plagioclase which have a solid solution series frequently form such crystals.

Zone of aeration: A zone between the land surface and the water table where pore spaces are filled mainly with air. Water that exists in the pore space in this zone is referred to as "soil moisture".

Zone of saturation: The zone beneath the water table where all pore spaces are completely filled with water. Water that exists within this zone is known as "ground water".

Zone of weathering: A subsurface area, above the water table, where mineral and organic materials are subject to weathering.

Zooplankton: The animal portion of plankton.

FORMULAE AND EQUATIONS:

GENERAL

Area

Area (A) of a circle with radius (r)

$$A = \pi r^2$$

Volume

Volume (V) of a sphere with radius (r)

$$V = \frac{4\pi r^3}{3}$$

Pressure in fluids

The pressure at a point in a fluid h metres below the surface is given by:

$$P = \rho g h$$

where:

P = pressure in pascals

ρ = density in kg/m^3

h = depth in metres

g = acceleration due to gravity = 9.8 m/sec^2

p_{at} is then equal to a head 10.3 metres of water.

AQUIFER PARAMETERS

Storage Coefficient (Storativity), (confined Aquifers) S

$$S = b\rho g(\beta\theta + \alpha(1-\theta))$$

$$= b\rho g(\frac{\theta}{E_w} + \frac{(1-\theta)}{E_s})$$

where:

b = thickness of the aquifer

ρ = density of the fluid (for water = 1,000 kg/m^3)

g = acceleration due to gravity

θ = porosity

β = compressibility of water, 4.8 x 10^{-7} kPa i.e.4.8 x 10^{-10} m^2/N

E_w = 1/β bulk modulus of water 2.08 x 10^6 kPa

α = compressibility of soil matrix. Sand and gravel α ~ 10^{-8} m^2/N

E_s = 1/α = bulk modulus of soil matrix

Specific mass storativity S_s

$$S_s = \frac{S}{b}$$

where:

S = Storage Coefficient

b = thickness of aquifer

Specific Mass Storativity has the dimensions length^{-1}.

It has the units metres^{-1}.

Hydraulic conductivity K

$$K = \frac{Q}{iA} = \frac{q}{i}$$

where:

Q = discharge rate through an area A

i = the hydraulic gradient

A = the cross-sectional area normal to the direction of flow

K = the hydraulic conductivity of the material

q = discharge per unit area

Average Hydraulic Conductivity in an isotropic medium

$$K_h av = \Sigma_{m=1}^{n} \frac{K_{hm} b_m}{b}$$

where:

K_{hav} = average horizontal hydraulic conductivity

K_{hm} = horizontal hydraulic conductivity of layer m

b_m = thickness of layer m

b = total thickness of all layers

Effective vertical hydraulic conductivity in an isotropic medium (K_v eff)

$$K_v eff = \frac{b}{\Sigma_{m=1}^{n} \dfrac{b_m}{K_{vm}}}$$

where:

$K_v eff$ = effective vertical hydraulic conductivity of all layers

K_{vm} = vertical hydraulic conductivity of layer m

b_m = thickness of layer m

b = combined thickness of all layers

Transmissivity (T)

$$T = Kb$$

where:

K = hydraulic conductivity

b = thickness of the aquifer

Hydraulic resistance (c)

$$c = \frac{b'}{K'}$$

where:

b^1 = the saturated thickness of the semi-pervious layer

K^1 = the vertical hydraulic conductivity of the semi-pervious layer

Leakage coefficient

LeakageCoefficient = K'/b'

where:

K' = vertical hydraulic conductivity of the semi-pervious layer

b'= saturated thickness of the semi-pervious layer

Leakage factor (L)

L = √(Kbc)

   = √(Tc)

where:

c = hydraulic resistance of the semi-pervious layer

K = hydraulic conductivity of the aquifer material

b = thickness of the aquifer

T = transmissivity of the aquifer

Drainage factor (B)

$$B = \sqrt{\frac{Kb}{\alpha S_y}}$$

or

$$B = \sqrt{\frac{T}{\beta S_y}}$$

where:

K = hydraulic conductivity of the aquifer

b = aquifer thickness

T = transmissivity of the aquifer

$1/\alpha$ = the Boulton delay index (an empirical constant)

S_y = the specific yield after a long pumping time

Large values of B indicate a fast drainage. If B = ∞ the yield is instantaneous with the lowering of the water table, so the aquifer would be confined without delayed yield.

The dimensions of B are in length, and the units are metres.

Barometric efficiency (BE)

$$BE = \rho g \Delta h / \Delta p_a$$

where:

ρ = density of water

g = gravitational acceleration

h = change in potentiometric level due to Δp_a

Δp_a = change in atmospheric pressure

The barometric efficiency can be interpreted as a measure of the competence of the overlying confining beds to resist pressure changes; thick impermeable confining strata are associated with high barometric efficiencies, whereas thinly confined aquifers will display low values.

The barometric efficiency of unconfined aquifers is zero, i.e. a change in atmospheric pressure does not result in a change in water level.

It can be shown that the barometric efficiency is related to the storage coefficient of an aquifer by the following equation:

$$S = \frac{\rho g b \theta}{E_w BE}$$

where:

S = storage coefficient

θ = porosity.

ρ = density of water

g = gravitational acceleration

b = thickness of the aquifer

E_w = bulk modulus of elasticity of water

BE = barometric efficiency

FLOW EQUATIONS

Darcy's Law

$$Q = KiA$$

where:

Q = rate of flow (in cubic metres per day)

i = hydraulic gradient or head loss per unit distance travelled (non dimensional)

A = the cross-sectional area through which the flow occurs (in square metres)

K = the coefficient of permeability or hydraulic conductivity (in metres/day)

Radius of influence for a pumping bore

$$r_0 = 1.5\sqrt{\frac{Tt}{S}}$$

where:

r_0 = radius of influence at time t after pumping commenced

T = transmissivity

t = time since pumping commenced

S = storage coefficient or specific yield, depending on the aquifer type

Thiem Equation for steady state flow (Confined Aquifer)

$$T = \frac{-2.3Q}{2\pi}\frac{\log_{10}(r_2/r_1)}{(s_1 - s_2)}$$

and

$$T = \frac{-2.3Q}{2\pi\Delta s'}$$

where:

T = transmissivity

Q = rate of flow (in cubic metres per day)

Δs' = drawdown per log cycle on the distance v drawdown plot

Theis equation for non-steady state flow (Confined Aquifer)

$$T = \frac{Q}{4\pi s} W(u)$$

where, in consistent units:

s = drawdown in an observation bore in the vicinity of the discharging bore, in metres

Q = the discharge rate (constant) of discharging bore, in cubic metres per day

T = transmissivity of the aquifer, in square metres per day

r = distance from discharging bore to observation bore, in metres

S = storage coefficient, expressed as a decimal fraction, dimensionless

t = time of discharge and observation, in days

u = lower limit of integration, $\qquad u = \dfrac{r^2 S}{4Tt}$

Jacob's modified non-steady state flow equation (Confined Aquifer)

s

$$= \frac{2.3Q}{4\pi s}(\log_{10}\frac{2.25Tt}{r^2 S})$$

$$T = \frac{2.3Q}{4\pi \Delta s}$$

$$S = \frac{2.25Tt_0}{r^2}$$

where:

s = drawdown in an observation bore in the vicinity of the discharging bore, in metres

Q = the discharge rate (constant) of discharging bore, in cubic metres per day

T = transmissivity of the aquifer, in square metres per day

r = distance from discharging bore to observation bore, in metres

S = storage coefficient, expressed as a decimal fraction, dimensionless

t = time from start of discharge, in days

t_0 = is point where of the "time-drawdown" curve intersects the zero drawdown line

Δs = drawdown per log cycle on the time/drawdown plot

Hantush-Jacob equation for radial flow (in a Leaky Aquifer)

$$s = \frac{Q}{4\pi T} L(u,v)$$

where:

L(u,v) is the well function for a leaky aquifer

$$u = \frac{r^2 S}{4Tt}$$
$$v = r/2L$$

L = the leakage factor

r = distance from the pumping bore

Boulton's equation (radial flow in an unconfined aquifer exhibiting delayed yield)

$$s = \frac{Q}{4\pi Kb} W(u_{AY}, r/B)$$

Refer to Hazel "Groundwater Hydraulics" Section 6.6.2

General equation for drawdown in a pumping bore

$$s_{wt} = (a + b\log t)Q + CQ^2$$

where:

s_{wt} = drawdown in the discharging bore at time "t" after discharge commenced

$$b = \frac{2.3}{4\pi T}$$

= a constant in most cases.

$$a = b\log\frac{2.25T}{r_w^2 S}$$

= a constant

C = a constant

T = transmissivity

Q = discharge rate

r_w = effective radius of the bore

t = time since discharge began at discharge rate Q

S = storage coefficient

Jacob's correction for drawdown in thin unconfined aquifers

s' = s - (s²/2b)

where:

s' = the corrected drawdown

s = the observed drawdown

b = the aquifer thickness

Jacob's correction for storage coefficient in thin unconfined aquifers

$$S = \frac{b-s}{b}S'$$

where:

S = the corrected value of Storage Coefficient

b = aquifer thickness

s = observed drawdown

S' = apparent storage coefficient calculated using corrected values of drawdown and Transmissivity

Eden-Hazel general drawdown equation during a variable discharge pumping test, such as a step drawdown test

$$s_{wt} = aQ_m + b\sum_{i=1}^{i=m} \log(t - t_i)\Delta Q_i + CQ_m^n$$

Refer to Section 7.4.6 of Hazel "Groundwater Hydraulics".

Hazel's Drawdown equation for intermittent pumping regime

$$S_{w,t=(n-1+p)} = F\Delta s + s_{w,t=p}$$

where:

$s_{w.(t=(n-1+p)}$ = the maximum drawdown to be expected during the nth time unit of intermittent pumping at discharge rate Q

p = fraction of the time unit for which pumping takes place

Δs = drawdown per log cycle of the "log time versus drawdown" curve for discharge rate Q

$s_{w,t=p}$ = drawdown at the end of the first pumping cycle. The inclusion of this term also accounts for the non-linear head loss during discharge

$$F = \log\frac{(n-1+p)!}{(n-1)!\,p}$$

Values of F have been computed for a number of "n" and "p". Curves of "F" versus "p", and "F" versus "n" for various "n" and "p" respectively have been plotted in **Figure 7-8** and **Figure 7-9** of Hazel "Groundwater Hydraulics".

Leakage

For vertical flow in the semi-confining layer or leaking layer Darcy's Law can be written as:

$$Q = -K^\mathsf{l} \frac{S}{b^\mathsf{l}} A$$

where:

K^l = vertical hydraulic conductivity of the semi-pervious layer

B^l = saturated thickness of the leaking layer

S = drawdown in the main aquifer

A = area through which leakage is occurring

Down valley flow

$$Q = TiW$$

where:

Q = total groundwater flow through the section considered

T = the average transmissivity in that section

i = the hydraulic gradient (i.e. the slope of the potentiometric surface)

W = width of the section being considered

Equations for flow net analysis

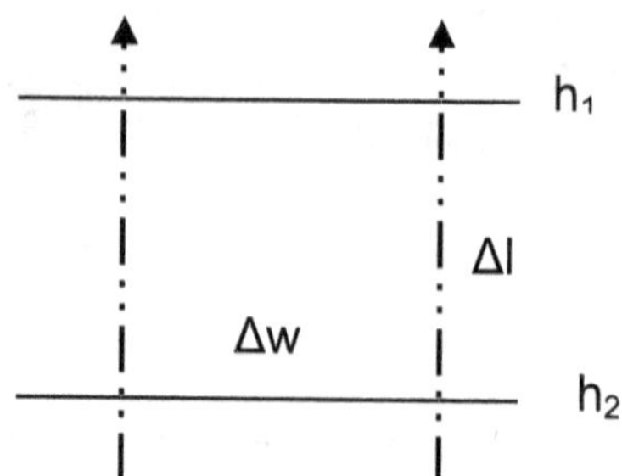

$$Q = -T \, (n_f/n_d)h$$

and

$$T = -\frac{Q}{(n_f / n_d)h}$$

where

n_f = number of flow channels

n_d = number of potential drops; and

Q = total flow

h = total head drop

STORAGE EQUATIONS

Total volume in storage

The total volume of water which is stored in a saturated material is given by:

$$V_T = V'_s \theta$$

where:

V_T = total volume of water stored

V's = total saturated volume

θ = porosity

Volumetric change in storage

Volume removed from or added to storage = S Δh

where:

S = storage coefficient for a confined aquifer

S = specific yield of dewatered material for any other type of aquifer

Δh = change in head during the period considered

SALTWATER INTRUSION EQUATIONS

Depth of the Interface

Hydrostatic conditions (Ghyben-Herzberg equation)

$$z = \frac{\rho_f}{(\rho_s - \rho_f)} h_f$$

where:

ρ_f = density of fresh water

ρ_s = density of salt water

h_f = head of fresh water above mean sea level

z = depth to the interface below mean sea level

Dynamic concept

$$z = \frac{\rho_s}{\rho_s - \rho_f} h_s - \frac{\rho_f}{\rho_s - \rho_f} h_f$$

where:

z = elevation at A above the datum level

ρ_f = density of fresh water

ρ_s = density of salt water

h_f = potentiometric head of fresh water

h_s = potentiometric head of salt water

Location of the interface

Confined aquifer

$$qL = \frac{K(\rho_s - \rho_f)}{2\rho_f} b^2$$

where:

q = discharge rate per unit width of aquifer

L = distance from shoreline to toe of wedge

K = hydraulic conductivity of aquifer

b = thickness of confined aquifer

ρ_f = density of fresh water

ρ_s = density of salt water

Unconfined aquifer

$$qL = \frac{Kb^2}{2}\frac{\rho_s}{\rho_f}(\rho_s - \rho_f)$$

or

$$qL = \frac{Tb}{2}\frac{\rho_s}{\rho_f}(\rho_s - \rho_f)$$

It can be seen from equation 11.14 and equation 11.10 that qL for an unconfined aquifer is ρ_s times qL for the confined aquifer.

where:

q = discharge rate per unit width of aquifer

L = length of wedge

K = hydraulic conductivity of the aquifer

T = transmissivity of the aquifer

b = saturated thickness

ρ_f = density of fresh water

ρ_s = density of salt water

MINE DEWATERING

Groundwater flow into a pit from each aquifer

Unconfined aquifer:

$$Q = \frac{\pi K(H^2 - h^2)}{2.3\log(r_0/r_w)} + 2\frac{(x+y)K(H^2 - h^2)}{2L_0}$$

Confined aquifer:

$$Q = \frac{2\pi K(H - h)}{2.3\log(r_0/r_w)} + 2\frac{(x+y)Kb(H - h)}{L_0}$$

where:

Q = discharge rate (m³/day)

K = hydraulic Conductivity (m/day)

H = potentiometric head in pit before pumping (m)

h_w = potentiometric head in pit during pumping (m)

h = potentiometric head at distance r from the pit (m)

r_0 = radius of cone of depression (radius of influence) (m)

r_w = effective radius of bore (say 1m) at corner quadrant (m)

= radial distance from pit (m)

L_0 = maximum length of drawdown influence from side of pit (use r_0) (m)

s = drawdown at distance r from the pit (m)

x = width of base of pit (m)

y = length of base of pit (m)

Metric Multiples

Symbol	Designation		Factor
T	tera-	10^{12}	1 000 000 000 000
G	giga	10^{9}	1 000 000 000
M	mega	10^{6}	1 000 000
k	kilo	10^{3}	1 000
h	hector	10^{2}	100
da	deca	10^{1}	10
d	deci	10^{-1}	0.1
c	centi	10^{-2}	0.01
m	milli	10^{-3}	0.001
µ	micro	10^{-6}	0.000 001
n	nano	10^{-9}	0.000 000 001
p	pico	10^{-12}	0.000 000 000 001

Greek Alphabet

Greek Character		Greek Name	English Equivalent	
Upper Case	Lower Case		Upper Case	Lower Case
A	α	alpha	A	a
B	β	beta	B	b
Γ	γ	gamma	G	g
Δ	δ	delta	D	d
E	ε	epsilon	Ĕ	ĕ
Z	ζ	zeta	Z	z
H	η	eta	Ē	ē
Θ	θ	theta	Th	th
I	ι	iota	I	i
K	κ	kappa	K	k
Λ	λ	lamda	L	l
M	µ	mu	M	m
N	ν	nu	N	n
Ξ	ξ	xi	X	x
O	o	omicron	Ŏ	ŏ
Π	π	pi	P	p
P	ρ	rho	R	r
Σ	σ	sigma	S	s
T	τ	tau	T	t
Y	υ	upsilon	Y	y

Φ	φ	phi	Ph	ph
Χ	χ	chi	Ch	ch
Ψ	ψ	psi	Ps	ps
Ω	ω	omega	Ō	ō

GEOLOGICAL TIMELINE

Precambrian Time: 4567 – 542 million years ago (mya))

Hadean Eon (4567 - 3800 mya)

- 4567 mya: Formation of the Solar System
- Sun was only 70% as bright as today
- 4500 mya: Formation of the Earth
- 4450 mya: The Moon accretes from fragments of a collision between the Earth and a planetoid
- Moon's orbit is beyond 64,000 km from the Earth
- Earth day is 7 hours long
- 4455 mya: Tidal locking causes one side of the Moon to face the Earth permanently
- Earth's original hydrogen and helium atmosphere escapes Earth's gravity
- 3900 mya: Cataclysmic meteorite bombardment
- The Moon is 282,000 km from Earth
- Earth day is 14.4 hours long
- Earth's atmosphere becomes mostly carbon dioxide, water vapour, methane, and ammonia
- Formation of carbonate minerals starts depleting atmospheric carbon dioxide
- There is no geologic record for the Hadean Eon

Archaean Eon (3800 – 2500 mya)

- 3800 mya: Surface of the Earth changed from molten to solid rock
- Water started condensing in liquid form
- Earth day is 15 hours long
- 3500 mya: Monocellular life started (Prokaryotes). First known oxygen-producing bacteria cyanobacteria (blue-green algae) form stromatolites
- 3000 mya: Atmosphere has 75% nitrogen, 15% carbon dioxide
- Sun brightens to 80% of current level
- Oldest record of Earth's magnetic field

Proterozoic Eon (2500 – 542 mya)

Paleoproterozoic Era (2500 – 1600 mya)

- Siderian Period (2500 – 2300 mya)
    - Stable continents first appeared
    - 2500 mya: First free oxygen is found in the oceans and atmosphere
    - 2400 mya: Great Oxidation Event, also called the Oxygen Catastrophe
    - Oxidation precipitates dissolved iron creating banded iron formations
    - Anaerobic organisms are poisoned by oxygen
    - 2400 mya: Start of Huronian ice age

- Rhyacian Period (2300 – 2050 mya)
    - 2200 mya: Organisms with mitochondria capable of aerobic respiration appear
    - 2100 mya: End of Huronian ice age

- Orosirian Period (2050 – 1800 mya)
    - Intensive mountain development (orogeny)
    - 2023 mya: Meteor impact, 300 km crater Vredefort, South Africa
    - 2000 mya: Solar luminosity is 85% of current level
    - Oxygen starts accumulating in the atmosphere
    - 1850 mya: Meteor impact, 250 km crater Sudbury, Ontario, Canada

- Statherian Period (1800 – 1600 mya)
    - Complex single-celled life appeared
    - Abundant bacteria and archaeans

Mesoproterozoic Era (1600 – 1000 mya)

- Calymmian Period (1600 – 1400 mya)
  - Photosynthetic organisms proliferate
  - Oxygen builds up in the atmosphere above 10%.
  - Formation of ozone layer starts blocking ultraviolet radiation from the sun
  - 1500 mya: Eukaryotic (nucleated) cells appear
- Ectasian Period (1400 – 1200 mya)
  - Green (Chlorobionta) and red (Rhodophyta) algae abound

- Stenian Period (1200 – 1000 mya)
  - 1200 mya: Spore/gamete formation indicates origin of sexual reproduction
  - 1100 mya: Formation of the supercontinent Rodinia

Neoproterozoic Era (1000 – 542 mya)

- Tonian Period (1000 – 850 mya)
  - 1000 mya: Multicellular organisms appear

Mesoproterozoic Era (1600 – 1000 mya)

- Calymmian Period (1600 – 1400 mya)
  - Photosynthetic organisms proliferate
  - 950 mya: Start of Stuartian-Varangian ice age
  - 900 mya: Earth day is 18 hours long
  - The Moon is 350,000 km from Earth

- Cryogenian Period (850 – 630 mya)
  - 750 mya: Breakup of Rodinia and formation of supercontinent Pannotia
  - 750 mya: End of last magnetic reversal
  - 650 mya: Mass extinction of 70% of dominant sea plants due to global glaciation ("Snowball Earth" hypothesis)
  - The Moon is 357,000 km from Earth

- Ediacaran (Vendian) Period (630 – 542 mya)
  - 600 may: Earth day is 20.7 hours long
  - 590 mya: Meteor impact, 90 km crater Acraman, South Australia
  - 580 mya: Soft-bodied organisms developed: Jellyfish, Tribrachidium, and Dickinsonia appeared
  - 570 mya: End of Stuartian-Varangian ice age
  - 550 mya: Pannotia fragmented into Laurasia and Gondwana

Phanerozoic Eon (542 mya – present)

Palaeozoic Era (542 – 251 mya)

- Cambrian Period (524 – 488.3 mya)
  - Abundance of multicellular life
  - Most of the major groups of animals first appear
  - Animals with shells appear
  - Solar brightness was 6% less than today

- Ordoviacian Period (488.3 – 443.7 mya)
  - Diverse marine invertebrates, such as trilobites, became common
  - First vertebrates appear in the ocean
  - First green plants and fungi on land

- o Fall in atmospheric carbon dioxide
- o 450 mya: Start of Andean-Saharan ice age
- o 443 mya: Glaciation of Gondwana super continent
- o Mass extinction of many marine invertebrates. Second largest mass extinction event. 49% of genera of fauna disappeared

- Silurian Period (443.7 – 416 mya)
    - o 420 mya: End of Andean-Saharan ice age
    - o Stablization of the earth's climate
    - o Coral reefs appeared
    - o First fish with jaws – sharks
    - o Insects (spiders, centipedes), and plants appear on land

- Devonian Period (416 – 359.2 mya)
    - o Ferns and seed-bearing plants (gymnosperms) appeared
    - o Formation of the first forests
    - o Earth day is ~21.8 hours long
    - o Wingless insects appeared on land
    - o 375 mya: Vertebrates with legs appeared
    - o Atmospheric oxygen level is about 16%
    - o First amphibians appear
    - o 374 mya: Mass extinction of 70% of marine species. This was a prolonged series of extinctions occurring over 20 million years. Evidence of anoxia in oceanic bottom waters, and global cooling. Surface temperatures dropped from about 34°C to about 26°C
    - o 359 mya: Meteor impact, 40 km crater Woodleigh, Australia

- Carboniferous Period (359.2 – 299 mya)

    - o Mississippian Epoch (359.2 – 299 mya)
        - ▪ Lower Carboniferous
        - ▪ 350 mya: Beginning of Karoo ice age

- - Large primitive trees develop
  - Forests consist of ferns, club mosses, horsetails, and gymnosperm
  - Oxygen levels increase
  - Vertebrates appear on land
  - First winged insects
  - Seas covered parts of the continents
  - 318 mya: Animals laying amniote eggs appear

  - Pennsylvanian Epoch (318.1 – 299 mya)
    - Upper Carboniferous
    - 310 mya: First reptiles
    - Atmospheric oxygen levels reach over 30%
    - Earth day is ~22.4 hours long
    - The Moon is 375,000 km from Earth
    - Giant arthropods populate the land
    - Transgression and regression of the seas caused by glaciations
    - Deposits of coal form in Europe, Asia, and North America

- Permian Period (299 – 251 mya)
  - 275 mya: Formation of the supercontinent
  - Conifers and cycads first appear
  - Earth is cold and dry
  - Sail-backed synapsids like *Edaphosaurus* and *Dimetrodon* appeared
  - 260 mya: End of Karoo ice age
  - 251 mya: Mass extinction (Permian-Triassic (P-T))
  - Possible 480km-wide meteor crater in the Wilkes Land region of Antarctica
  - Period of great volcanism in Siberia releases large volume of gases (CO_2, CH_4, and H_2S)
  - Oxygen (O_2) levels dropped from 30% to 12% Carbon dioxide (CO_2) level was about 2000 ppm

- o Earth's worst mass extinction eliminated 90% of ocean dwellers, and 70% of land plants and animals

Mesozoic Era (251 – 65.56 mya)

- Triassic Period (251 – 199.6 mya)
    - o Break up of Panaea super continent starts
    - o Survivors of P-T extinction spread and recolonise
    - o Reptiles populate the land
    - o 240 mya: Sea urchins (*Arkarua*) appear
    - o 235 mya: Evolutionary split between dinosaurs and lizards
    - o Giant marine *ichthyosaurs* and *plesiosaurs* populate the seas
    - o First small dinosaurs such as *celophysis* appear on land
    - o 225 may*: Adelobasileus* proto-mammal emerged
    - o 214 mya: Meteor impact, 100 km crater Manicouagan, Quebec, Canada
    - o 205 mya: First evidence of mammals: *Morganucodon*
    - o 201 mya: Mass extinction caused by oceanic anoxic event killed 20% of all marine families

- Jurassic Period (199.6 – 145.5 mya)
    - o Earth is warm and there is no polar ice.
    - o Age of the dinosaurs
    - o Giant herbivores and vicious carnivores dominate the land
    - o Flying reptiles (Pterosaurs) appeared
    - o 180 mya: North America separates from Africa
    - o 167 mya: Meteor impact, 80 km crater Puchezh-Katunki, Russia
    - o 166 mya: Evolutionary split of monotremes from primitive mammals
    - o 150 mya: First birds like *Archaeopteryx* appear
    - o 148 mya: Evolutionary split between marsupial and eutherian mammals

- o 145 mya: Meteor impact, 70 km crater Morokweng, South Africa

- Cretaceous Period (145.5 – 65.5 mya)
  - o Period of active crust plate movements
  - o 133 mya: Meteor impact, 55 km crater Tookoonooka, Australia
  - o 125 mya: Africa and India separate from Antarctica
  - o 120 mya: Global warming event starts. Carbon dioxide levels were 550 to 590 ppm
  - o Flowering plants (angiosperms) appeared
  - o 110 mya: Crocodiles appeared
  - o 105 mya: South America breaks away from Africa
  - o Formation of the Atlantic Ocean
  - o Earth has no polar ice
  - o Modern mammals and birds developed
  - o 100 mya: Earth's magnetic field is 3 times stronger than today
  - o 90 mya: Global warming event ends
  - o 70 mya: Meteor impact, 65 km crater Kara, Russia
  - o 68 mya: Tyrannosaurus rex thrived
  - o 67 mya: Deccan Traps volcanic eruptions start in India and produce great volume of lava and gases
  - o 65.5 mya: Meteor impact, 170 km crater Chicxulub, Yucatan, Mexico
  - o Mass extinction of 80-90% of marine species and 85% of land species, including the dinosaurs

Cenozoic Era (65.5 mya – present day)

- Palaeogene Period (65.5 – 23.03 mya)

- Tertiary Period (65.5 – 2.58 mya)

  - o Palaeocene Epoch (65.5 – 55.8 mya)
    - ▪ 63 mya: End of Deccan Traps volcanic eruptions in India

- Appearance of placental mammals (marsupials, insectivores, lemuroids, creodonts)
- Flowering plants become widespread
- 60 mya: Earliest known ungulate (hoofed mammal)
- Formation of the Rocky Mountain
- 55.8 mya: Major global warming episode
- North Pole temperature averaged 23°C (73.4°F), CO_2 concentration was 2000 ppm

- Eocene Epoch (55.8 – 33.9 mya)
  - 50 mya: India meets Asia, forming the Himalayas
  - 45 mya: Australia separates from Antarctica
  - Earth day is 24 hours long
  - The Moon is 378,000 km from Earth
  - Modern mammals appear: rhinoceros, camels, early horses appear
  - 35.6 mya: Meteor impacts, 90 and 100 km craters Chesapeake Bay, Virginia, USA, and Popigai, Russia
  - 34 mya: Global cooling creates permanent Antarctic ice sheet

- Oligocene Epoch (33.9 – 23.03 mya)
  - Appearance of many grasses
  - First elephants with trunks
  - 27.8 mya: La Garita, Colorado supervolcanic eruption

- Neocene Period (23.03 mya – present day)
  - Miocene Epoch (23.03 – 5.3 mya)
    - African-Arabian plate joined Asia
    - 14 mya: Antarctica separates from Australia and South America
      circum-polar ocean circulation builds up Antarctic ice cap
    - Warmer global climates
    - First raccoons appear

- Drying of continental interiors
- Forests give way to grasslands
- 6 mya: Upright walking (bipedal) hominins appear

- Pliocene Epoch (5.3 – 2.58 mya)
  - 4.4 mya: Appearance of Ardipithecus, an early hominin genus
  - 4 mya: North and South America join at the Isthmus of Panama
  - Animals and plants cross the new land bridge
  - Ocean currents change in the newly isolated Atlantic Ocean
  - 3.9 mya: Appearance of *Australopithecus*, genus of hominids
  - 3.7 mya: *Australopithecus* hominids inhabit Eastern and Northern Africa
  - 3 mya: Formation of Arctic ice cap
  - Accumulation of ice at the poles
  - Climate became cooler and drier
  - Spread of grasslands and savannas
  - Rise of long-legged grazing animals

- Quaternary Period (2.58 – present day)
  - Pleistocene Epoch (2.58 – 11,400 years ago)
    - Several major episodes of global cooling, or glaciations
    - 2.4 mya: *Homo habilis* appeared
    - 2.1 mya: Yellowstone supervolcanic eruption
    - 2 mya: Tool-making humanoids emerge
    - Beginning of the Stone Age
    - 1.7 mya: *Homo erectus* first moves out of Africa
    - 1.3 mya: Yellowstone supervolcanic eruption
    - 1.3 mya to 820,000 yrs ago: Sherwin Glaciation
    - Presence of large land mammals and birds
    - 700,000 yrs ago: Human and Neanderthal lineages start to diverge genetically
    - 680,000 to 620,000 yrs ago: Günz/Nebraskan glacial period

- 640,000 yrs ago: Yellowstone supervolcanic eruption
- 530,000 yrs ago: Development of speech in *Homo Heidelbergensis*
- 455,000 to 300,000 yrs ago: Mindel/Kansan glacial period
- 400,000 yrs ago: Hominids hunt with wooden spears and use stone cutting tools
- 370,000 yrs ago: Human ancestors and Neanderthals are fully separate populations
- 300,000 yrs ago: Hominids use controlled fires
- Neanderthal man spreads through Europe 230,000 yrs ago
- 200,000 to 130,000 yrs ago: Riss/Illinoian glacial period
- 160,000 yrs ago: *Homo sapiens* appeared
- Origin of human female lineage (Mitochondrial Eve)
- 125,000 yrs ago: Eemian stage or Riss/Würm interglacial period
- Hardwood forests grew above the Arctic Circle
- Melting ice sheets increased sea level by 6 meters
- 110,000 yrs ago: Start of Würm/Wisconsin glacial period
- 105,000 yrs ago: Stone Age humans forage for grass seeds such as sorghum
- 80,000 yrs ago: Non-African humans interbreed with Neanderthals
- 74,000 yrs ago: Toba volcanic eruption releases large volume of sulphur dioxide
- *Homo sapiens* reduced to about 10,000 individuals
- 70,000 yrs ago: *Tahoe* glacial maximum glaciers cover Canada and northern US
- 60,000 yrs ago: Oldest male ancestor of modern humans
- 46,000 yrs ago: Australia becomes arid, bush fires destroy habitat, and megafauna die off
- 40,000 yrs ago: *Cro-Magnon* man appeared in Europe
- 28,000 yrs ago: Neanderthals disappear from fossil record

- 26,500 yrs ago: Taupo supervolcanic eruption in New Zealand
- 22,000 yrs ago: *Tioga* glacial maximum sea level was 130 meters lower than today
- 19,000 yrs ago: Antarctic sea ice starts melting.
- 15,000 yrs ago: Bering land bridge between Alaska and Siberia allows human migration to America
- 12,900 yrs ago: Explosion of comet over Canada causes extinction of American megafauna such as the mammoth and sabre tooth cat (*Smilodon*), as well as the end of Clovis culture
- Fired pottery invented (12,000 yrs ago)
- 11,400 yrs ago: End of Würm/Wisconsin glacial period
- Sea level rises by 91 meters

- Holocene Epoch (11,400 years ago – present day)
  - Development of agriculture
  - Domestication of animals
  - 9,000 yrs ago: Metal smelting began
  - 5,500 yrs ago: Invention of the wheel
  - 5,300 yrs ago: The Bronze Age
  - 5,000 yrs ago: Development of writing
  - 4,500 yrs ago: Pyramids of Giza3,300 yrs ago: The Iron Age
  - 2,230 yrs ago: Archimedes advances mathematics
  - 250 yrs ago: Start of the Industrial Revolution
  - 50 yrs ago: Space travel
  - Artificial satellite orbits the earth
  - Humans walk on the moon
  - And so it continues...

NOTE: One way to grasp the magnitude of geological time is to compare it to the events in a year, to compress the entire 4.6 billion years into 365 days. On that scale the oldest rocks we can date formed about mid-March, and we find living creatures such as algae and jellyfish in May. Plants and then animals did not emerge on land until the end of November, and the valuable coal basins of eastern Australia were formed from vast peatlands over a period of 19 hours on 10 December. Dinosaurs roamed central Queensland from shortly after this until 26 December, when Australia separated from Antarctica and started its drift northwards towards Asia. The Great Barrier Reef probably formed mainly after 11.03 pm on 31 December. Aboriginal people arrived perhaps around 11.54 pm, and the last of the giant kangaroos died out by 11:59:35. At twenty five seconds to go, Rome ruled the Western world for 5 seconds from 11:59:45 to 11:59:50. James Cook arrived on the Australian coast at one second to midnight. And, as they say, the rest is history.

Geological time scale at a glance:

Era	Period	Epoch	Age (mya)
Cenozoic	Quaternary	Holocene	0.01
		Pleistocene	1.8
	Tertiary	Pliocene	5.3
		Miocene	23.8
		Oligocene	33.7
		Eocene	55
		Palaeocene	65
Mesozoic	Cretaceous		145
	Jurassic		200
	Triassic		251
Palaeozoic	Permian		299

	Carboniferous		359
	Devonian		417
	Silurian		443
	Ordovician		490
	Cambrian		542
Precambrian			4600

Reference List:

Importance of Groundwater:

Physical and Chemical Hydrogeology. Domenico, PA and Schwartz, FW

ISBN-10: 0471597627

Applied Hydrogeology (4th edition). Fetter, CW

ISBN: 0130882399

Groundwater. Freeze, RA and Cherry, JA

ISBN: 0133653129

Groundwater and Geologic Processes. Ingebritsen, S; Sanford, W and Neuzil, C

ISBN: 0521603218

Introducing Groundwater. Price, M

ISBN: 0412485001

Groundwater in the Environment. Younger, P

ISBN: 1405121432

Groundwater Hydrology. Todd, DK and Mays, LW

ISBN: 0471059374

A Manual of Field Hydrogeology. Saunders, LL

ISBN: 0132279274

Groundwater Storage:

Analysis and Evaluation of Pumping Test Data. Kruseman, GP and de Ridder, NA

ASIN: B0059NAG2K

Groundwater Hydraulics. Hazel, Colin

Available from: www.srit.com.au

The Geology of Australia. Jonson, D

ISBN: 0521767415

Groundwater Extraction:

Minimum Construction Requirements for Water Bores in Australia.
Land & Water Biodiversity Committee

www.adit.com.au

Groundwater and Wells (2nd edition 1986, 3rd edition 2010). Driscoll

ISBN: 0978779304

Seepage, Drainage & Flownets. Cedergren, HR

ISBN: 047118053X

Hydrometric Determinations – Pumping tests for waterwells.
Considerations and guidelines for design, performance and use. ISO
14686:2003

ASIN: B000Y2UCPC

Pumping Test Analyses: Case-studies in Groundwater Resource
Evaluation. Jones, GP and Rushton, KR

Minimum Construction Requirements for Water Bores in Australia (2nd
edition). Land and Water Biodiversity Committee. 2003

Groundwater and Wells (2nd edition) Sterrett, RJ

ISBN: 0978779304

Minimum Construction Requirements for Water Bores in Australia (3rd Edition Feb 2012)

Refer www.aditc.com.au

Groundwater Chemistry:

Environmental Applications of Geochemical Modelling. Zhu, C and Anderson, G

ISBN: 0521005779

Aqueous Environmental Geochemistry. Langmuir, D

ISBN: 0023674121

The Geochemistry of Natural Waters – Surface and Groundwater Environments (3rd edition). Drever, J

ISBN: 132727900

Aquatic Chemistry: An Introduction Emphasizing Chemical Eqilibria in Natural Waters. Stumm, W and Morgan JJ

ISBN: 0471091731

Groundwater Management:

State Water Acts

Groundwater (Border Agreement) Act 1985

www.austill.edu.au/au/legis/vic/consol_act/gaa1985291/

COAG 1996 Allocation and Use of Groundwater Occasional Paper2.

Basin Salinity Strategy

www.mdbc.gov.au/salinity/basin_salinity_management_strategy_20012015amrcainz

Groundwater Protection Act 1970

SEPP Groundwaters of Victoria

www.epa.vic.gov.au/about_us/legislation/land.asp#sepp_ground waters

Groundwater Trading Websites:

www.watermove.com.au

www.waterexchange.com.au

Groundwater Protection:

Pesticide Impact Rating Index. CSIRO Australia

www.csiro.au

A Guide to the use of Pesticides in Western Australia (2010).
Department of Health (WA)

www.health.wa.gov.au

Public Service Circular 88: Use of herbicides in water catchment
areas. Department of Health (WA)

www.health.wa.gov.au

Statewide Policy No. 2: Pesticide use in public drinking water source
areas (2000). Department of Water

www.water.wa.gov.au

Footprint (Europe)

www.eu-footprint.org/index.html

General information on pesticides (toxicology). Cooperative effort including: University of California-Davis; Oregon State University; Michigan State University; Cornell University; University of Idaho

www.extoxnet.orst.edu

Contaminant Hydrogeology. Fetter, CW

ISBN: 157766583X

Computer Modelling

Groundwater Flow Modelling Guideline. Murray Darling Basin Commission (2000). National Water Commission (2011)

ISBN: 1876830166

Surface Water Management

Natural Channel Design

Upload onto SRIT Website.

Miscellaneous Web sites

Department of Environment & Resource Management (DERM/QLD)
Interactive Water Monitoring Data Portal

www.watermonitoring.derm.qld.gov.au/host.htm

Australian Bureau of Meteorology

www.bom.gov.au

United States Geological Survey

www.usgs.gov

Groundwater Ambient Network (EPA/QLD)

www.epa.qld.gov.au/wetlandinfo/site/supporttools/monitoringextentandcondition/current-and-future-monitoring/groundwater-ambient-network.html

Groundwater Level Network (EPA/QLD)

www.epa.qld.gov.au/wetlandinfo/site/supporttools/monitoringextentandcondition/current-and-future-monitoring/groundwater-level-network-wq.html

Great Artesian Basin Springs Monitoring Program (EPA/QLD)

www.epa.qld.gov.au/wetlandinfo/site/supporttools/monitoringextentandcondition/current-and-future-monitoring/great-artesian-basin-springs-monitoring-program.html

Periodic Table

Atomic Number	Atomic Weight	Name	Symbol	Atomic Number	Atomic Weight	Name	Symbol
1	1.0079	Hydrogen	H	31	69.723	Gallium	Ga
2	4.0026	Helium	He	32	72.64	Germanium	Ge
3	6.941	Lithium	Li	33	74.9216	Arsenic	As
4	9.0122	Beryllium	Be	34	78.96	sElenium	Se
5	10.811	Boron	B	35	79.904	Bromine	Br
6	12.0107	Carbon	C	36	83.8	Krypton	Kr
7	14.0067	Nitrogen	N	37	85.4678	Rubidium	Rb
8	15.9994	Oxygen	O	38	87.62	Strontium	Sr
9	18.9984	Fluorine	F	39	88.9059	Yttrium	Y
10	20.1797	Neon	Ne	40	91.224	Zirconium	Zr
11	22.9897	Sodium	Na	41	92.9064	Niobium	Nb
12	24.305	Magnesium	Mg	42	95.94	Molybdenum	Mo
13	26.9815	Aluminium	Al	43	~98	Technetium	Tc
14	28.0855	Silicon	Si	44	107.07	Rutherium	Ru
15	30.9738	Phosphorus	P	45	102.9055	Rhodium	Rh
16	32.065	Sulphur	S	46	106.42	Palladium	Pd
17	35.453	Chlorine	Cl	47	107.8682	Silver	Ag
18	39.948	Argon	Ar	48	112.411	Cadmium	Cd
19	39.098	Potassium	K	49	114.818	Indium	In

Glossary of Terms

20	40.078	Calcium	Ca	50	118.71	Tin	Sn
21	44.9559	Scandium	Sc	51	121.76	Antimony	Sb
22	47.867	Titanium	Ti	52	127.6	Tellurium	Te
23	50.9415	Vanadium	V	53	126.9045	Iodine	I
24	51.9961	Chromium	Cr	54	131.293	Xenon	Xe
25	54.938	Manganese	Mn	55	132.9055	Cesium	Cs
26	55.845	Iron	Fe	56	137.327	Barium	Ba
27	58.9332	Cobalt	Co	57	138.9055	Lanthanum	La
28	58.6934	Nickle	Ni	58	140.116	Cerium	Ce
29	63.546	Copper	Cu	59	140.9077	Prasodymium	Pr
30	65.39	Zinc	Zn	60	144.24	Neodymium	Nd

Periodic Table (cont.)

Atomic Number	Atomic Weight	Name	Symbol	Atomic Number	Atomic Weight	Name	Symbol
61	~145	Promethium	Pm	91	231.0359	Protactium	Pa
62	150.36	Samarium	Sm	92	238.0289	Uranium	U
63	151.964	Europium	Eu	93	~237	Neptunium	Np
64	157.25	Gadolinium	Gd	94	~244	Plutonium	Pu
65	158.9253	Terbium	Tb	95	~243	Americium	Am
66	162.5	Dysprosium	Dy	96	~247	Curium	Cm
67	164.9	Holmium	Ho	97	~247	Berkelium	Bk

	303	m				m	
68	167.259	Erbium	Er	98	~251	Californium	Cf
69	168.259	Thulium	Tm	99	~252	Einsteinium	Es
70	173.04	Ytterbium	Yb	100	~257	Fermium	Fm
71	174.967	Lutetium	Lu	101	~258	Mendelevium	Md
72	178.49	Hafnium	Hf	102	~259	Nobelium	No
73	180.9479	Tatalum	Ta	103	~262	Lawrencium	Lr
74	183.84	Tungsten	W	104	~261	Rutherfordium	Rf
75	186.207	Rhenium	Re	105	~262	Dubnium	Db
76	190.23	Osmium	Os	106	~266	Seaborgium	Sg
77	192.217	Iridium	Ir	107	~264	Bohrium	Bh
78	195.078	Platinum	Pt	108	~277	Hassium	Hs
79	196.9665	Gold	Au	109	~268	Meitnerium	Mt
80	200.59	Mercury	Hg	110	~281	Darmstadtium	Ds
81	204.3833	Thallium	Tl	111	~282	Roentgenium	Rg
82	207.2	Lead	Pb	112	~285	Copernicium	Cn
83	208.9804	Bismuth	Bi	113	~285	Ununtrium	Uut
84	~209	Polonium	Po	114	~289	Flerovium	Fl
85	~210	Astatine	At	115	~289	Ununpentium	Uup
86	~222	Radon	Rn	116	~293	Livermorium	Lv
87	~223	Francium	Fr	117	~294	Ununseptium	Uus
88	~226	Radium	Ra	118	~294	Ununocti	Uuo

						um	
89	~227	Actinium	Ac				
90	232.0391	Thorium	Th				

v

9 781976 977138